IMMERSION
Bible Studies

EZRA
NEHEMIAH
ESTHER

Weeds
something growing where you
don't want it –
    Claudia's orig planting
forgiveness = God
    Linda's father

Praise for IMMERSION

"IMMERSION BIBLE STUDIES is a powerful tool in helping readers to hear God speak through Scripture and to experience a deeper faith as a result."
  Adam Hamilton, author of *24 Hours That Changed the World*

"IMMERSION BIBLE STUDIES is a godsend for participants who desire sound Bible study yet feel they do not have large amounts of time for study and preparation. IMMERSION is concise. It is brief but covers the material well and leads participants to apply the Bible to life. IMMERSION is a wonderful resource for today's church."
  Larry R. Baird, senior pastor of Trinity Grand Island United Methodist Church

"If you're looking for a deeper knowledge and understanding of God's Word, you must dive into IMMERSION BIBLE STUDIES. Whether in a group setting or as an individual, you will experience God and his unconditional love for each of us in a whole new way."
  Pete Wilson, founding and senior pastor of Cross Point Church

"This beautiful series helps readers become fluent in the words and thoughts of God, for purposes of illumination, strength building, and developing a closer walk with the One who loves us so."
  Laurie Beth Jones, author of *Jesus, CEO* and *The Path*

"The IMMERSION BIBLE STUDIES series is no less than a game changer. It ignites the purpose and power of Scripture by showing us how to do more than just know God or love God; it gives us the tools to love like God as well."
  Shane Stanford, author of *You Can't Do Everything . . . So Do Something*

IMMERSION
Bible Studies

EZRA
NEHEMIAH
ESTHER

Stan Purdum

Abingdon Press

Nashville

EZRA, NEHEMIAH, ESTHER
IMMERSION BIBLE STUDIES
by Stan Purdum

Library of Congress Cataloging-in-Publication Data

Purdum, Stan, 1945-
    Ezra, Nehemiah, Esther : Immersion Bible studies / by Stan Purdum.
        pages cm
    ISBN 978-1-4267-1636-2 (curriculum—printed text plus-cover : alk. paper) 1. Bible.
O.T. Ezra—Meditations. 2. Bible. O.T. Nehemiah—Meditations. 3. Bible. O.T.
Esther—Meditations. I. Title.
    BS1355.54.P87 2012
    222'.06—dc23

                                                                        2012030073

Editor: Jan Turrentine
Leader Guide Writer: Jan Turrentine

12 13 14 15 16 17 18 19 20 21—10 9 8 7 6 5 4 3 2 1

Manufactured in the United States of America

Contents

Review Team

Diane Blum
Pastor
East End United Methodist Church
Nashville, Tennessee

Susan Cox
Pastor
McMurry United Methodist Church
Claycomo, Missouri

Margaret Ann Crain
Professor of Christian Education
Garrett-Evangelical Theological Seminary
Evanston, Illinois

Nan Duerling
Curriculum Writer and Editor
Cambridge, Maryland

Paul Escamilla
Pastor and Writer
St. John's United Methodist Church
Austin, Texas

James Hawkins
Pastor and Writer
Smyrna, Delaware

Andrew Johnson
Professor of New Testament
Nazarene Theological Seminary
Kansas City, Missouri

Snehlata Patel
Retired Pastor
Brooklyn, New York

Emerson B. Powery
Professor of New Testament
Messiah College
Grantham, Pennsylvania

Clayton Smith
Pastoral Staff
Church of the Resurrection
Leawood, Kansas

Harold Washington
Professor of Hebrew Bible
Saint Paul School of Theology
Kansas City, Missouri

Carol Wehrheim
Curriculum Writer and Editor
Princeton, New Jersey

IMMERSION BIBLE STUDIES

A fresh new look at the Bible, from beginning to end,
and what it means in your life.

Welcome to IMMERSION!

We've asked some of the leading Bible scholars, teachers, and pastors to help us with a new kind of Bible study. IMMERSION remains true to Scripture but always asks, "Where are you in your life? What do you struggle with? What makes you rejoice?" Then it helps you read the Scriptures to discover their deep, abiding truths. IMMERSION is about God and God's Word, and it is also about you—not just your thoughts, but your feelings and your faith.

In each study you will prayerfully read the Scripture and reflect on it. Then you will engage it in three ways:

Claim Your Story
> Through stories and questions, think about your life, with its struggles and joys.

Enter the Bible Story
> Explore Scripture and consider what God is saying to you.

Live the Story
> Reflect on what you have discovered, and put it into practice in your life.

IMMERSION makes use of an exciting new translation of Scripture, the Common English Bible (CEB). The CEB and IMMERSION BIBLE STUDIES will offer adults:
- the emotional expectation to find the love of God
- the rational expectation to find the knowledge of God
- reliable, genuine, and credible power to transform lives
- clarity of language

Whether you are using the Common English Bible or another translation, IMMERSION BIBLE STUDIES will offer a refreshing plunge into God's Word, your life, and your life with God.

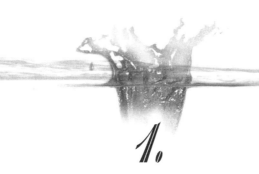

1.

Help From Surprising Sources

Ezra 1:1–4:5; 4:24–6:22

Claim Your Story

Not long after my wife became pregnant with our first child, she awoke one morning with severe pain in her abdomen. I rushed her to the hospital where she was seen first by an emergency room doctor and then by a surgeon. The surgeon concluded Jeanine's pain was likely from an ectopic pregnancy, an embryo that had established itself in a fallopian tube instead of the uterus. Surgery was necessary, he said, and assuming it was an ectopic pregnancy, he would have to remove the fallopian tube, which would also end the pregnancy. We should be prepared for that likelihood, he said.

Jeanine underwent the procedure, and as it turned out, the embryo was in the right place, but one of the fallopian tubes was strangulated. The surgeon untangled it and closed the incision. When this doctor talked to us later, he explained that because of Jeanine's innards being disturbed, it was now likely that the pregnancy would spontaneously abort. The physician then left the room.

While Jeanine and I began to absorb this unwelcome prediction, our family doctor walked in. He agreed that the surgery had been necessary, but when we told him what the surgeon had said about the likely loss of the pregnancy, he said, "I think the odds are better than that. There's a lot of resilience there."

We clung to those words, not only because they were what we wanted to hear, but also because we knew something about our doctor's faith. He had a sign in his waiting room that read, "We dress the wound, but God heals." When I once commented to him about that, he responded with a specific mention of his commitment to Christ.

As it turned out, the pregnancy continued, and at full term, the family doctor delivered our healthy baby son.

Naturally, Jeanine and I had prayed before she went to surgery. While our own physician—a practicing Christian—brought hope into the hospital room that day, the surgeon—an abrupt man who gave no hint of his religious persuasion—was the direct provider of Jeanine's medical salvation and the one who cleared the way for the pregnancy to continue. As far as we were concerned, God worked through *both* of these men.

In the more than thirty-five years since, Jeanine and I and the three children who eventually rounded out our family have all had occasional medical issues, a few of them quite serious, and we have had the services of a variety of physicians. Only now and then were we aware of being treated by someone who was a committed Christian. Sometimes we recognized that particular doctors were members of other religions. Nonetheless, we often felt that God used medical practitioners from all these religious (and occasionally nonreligious) backgrounds to answer our prayers for healing.

You've probably had similar experiences, if not in medicine, then perhaps in legal matters, education, business, transportation, employment, or some other field. You may have even perceived an answer to prayer when a member of your family married someone of another faith—or no faith— who proved to be a devoted spouse and parent.

If you've read the Book of Ezra before, it should come as no surprise that God works through both believers and unbelievers to accomplish God's purposes, for this biblical book contains two prime examples: It was the Persian king Cyrus, an unbeliever, who made it possible for the Jews in exile in Babylonia to return to their homeland and start rebuilding their temple. It was one of his successors, Darius, another unbeliever, who enabled them to finish the job.

Now, as then, God's purposes are not derailed simply because there's no believer in the driver's seat.

Enter the Bible Story

The books of Ezra and Nehemiah are the final installments in the Old Testament storyline. That story began with God's call of Abraham (Genesis

12) and was followed by the time of the patriarchs (Genesis 12–50). It continued through Israel's wilderness period (Exodus through Deuteronomy), the conquest and settlement of Canaan and the pre-monarchy (Joshua; Judges; 1 Samuel 1–8), the monarchy (1 Samuel 9–31; 2 Samuel; 1 Kings 1–11; 1 Chronicles 10–29; 2 Chronicles 1–9), the divided kingdom (1 Kings 12–22; 2 Kings 1–24; 2 Chronicles 10–36), and the fall of Jerusalem and Babylonian exile (2 Kings 25; 2 Chronicles 36). Ezra and Nehemiah complete the story, telling of the return of the exiles and the rebuilding of Jerusalem. There are more Old Testament books following Nehemiah, to be sure—in fact, those by the prophets plug into the Genesis-to-Nehemiah storyline—but none move that storyline any further in time beyond the end of Nehemiah.

Cyrus, Agent of God (Ezra 1)

The Book of Ezra opens by saying King Cyrus of Persia was in his first year of rule (1:1), but in reality, he had already been the monarch of the Persian Empire for twenty years. It was, however, Cyrus's first year as ruler over the Babylonians, having defeated their army and added their country to the Persian realm. From the viewpoint of the people of Judah living in forced exile in that conquered land, Cyrus's takeover launched a new era, and his reign was "year one" of that era.

Cyrus's victory was good news for the exiles because unlike the Babylonian kings, Cyrus was quite willing for subject peoples to live in their own lands and worship their own gods. He was even willing for the empire to help fund their places of worship. This apparent magnanimity may have arisen from a pluralistic outlook on Cyrus's part—a willingness to thank "whatever gods there may be" for his success as well as seek their blessing on his continuing endeavors. But it was also politically expedient, helping to garner gratitude and loyalty from subject peoples throughout his realm.

Whatever Cyrus's motivations, the unidentified Hebrew prophet whose messages to the exiled Jews appear in Isaiah 40–55 announced in advance that Cyrus would be God's "shepherd" who would do what God wanted (44:28). This prophet also referred to Cyrus as the Lord's "anointed"

(45:1) and quoted God as saying, "I have a right to awaken Cyrus; / I will smooth all his paths. / He will build my city and set my exiles free" (45:13).

During that "first year," Cyrus issued a proclamation saying that Israel's God had commanded him to "build him a house at Jerusalem in Judah" (Ezra 1:2). His proclamation granted permission for any Jewish exiles who wished to go to Judah to do so with both his blessing and the monetary and commodities support of those Jews who preferred to stay in Babylonia.

This proclamation appears twice in Ezra, first in 1:2-4, where it was originally in Hebrew, and again in 6:3-5, where it was originally in Aramaic. There are some differences in the two, which may have been because the Hebrew version gives the oral proclamation of the king's herald, while the Aramaic version was the official written memorandum of the decree. One difference is that the Hebrew version makes it sound as if the cost of the Temple rebuilding was to be entirely from the gifts given by the Jews remaining behind, while the Aramaic version clearly states, "The cost will be paid from the royal treasury" (6:4). Probably both sources helped fund the project. And in any case, those Jews not making the trek readily assisted those going to Judah "with silver equipment, with gold, with goods, livestock, and valuable gifts, in addition to all that was freely

---

About the Scripture

How Long Was the Exile?

Both Jeremiah (29:10) and the author of 2 Chronicles (36:21) say that the Exile would last seventy years, yet the dates from the three known deportations (598, 586, and 582 B.C.—see Jeremiah 52:28-30) to Cyrus's decree freeing the exiles (537 B.C.) work out to sixty-one, forty-nine, and forty-five years, respectively. Some Bible scholars suggest there was a previous deportation in 605 at the time when Judah first became a vassal nation to Babylonia, but even that yields only sixty-eight years. That's close enough to round upward to seventy, but it's more likely that the biblical writers were using seventy in a metaphorical way. In biblical numerology, seventy, a multiple of seven (as in the six days of Creation and the seventh day when God rested) signifies completeness. In other words, the biblical writers were telling the people that their time of exile would be a full measure.

offered" (1:6). What's more, Cyrus gave the homeland-bound group the fixtures and treasures from the original Temple, items that the Babylonians had plundered from it at the time they had destroyed it.

Those Who Returned (Ezra 2)

It was a sizable group that made the trek from Babylonia to Judah—nearly fifty thousand people when you total the numbers in Ezra 2:64-65—and they were led by Sheshbazzar, who had been appointed by Cyrus for the task. Ezra 1:8 describes Sheshbazzar as "the prince of Judah," and it's probable that he was a son of Jehoiachin, the king of Judah who was deported to Babylonia in 598 B.C. (see 2 Chronicles 36:9-10). Jehoiachin's sons are listed in 1 Chronicles 3:18 (where Jehoiachin is called Jeconiah) and it's possible that the son there called Shenazzar was Sheshbazzar. This would also make Sheshbazzar a descendant of King David. Cyrus appointed him to be governor of Judah upon his arrival there (Ezra 5:14).

In the Common English Bible, the heading above Ezra 2 is "List of the returnees," but most of the fifty thousand people who "went up from there" (2:1) were not literally "returnees," for most had been born in Babylonia and had never even seen Judah. They were returnees only in the sense they that they were heading for the homeland of their ancestors.

Judging from the report in Jeremiah 52:28-30, the largest group of captives had been taken from Judah to Babylonia in 598 B.C. at the same time Jehoiachin was deported. A smaller group was marched out when the Babylonian army destroyed Jerusalem in 586, and a few hundred more were deported in 582, possibly as punishment for disturbance surrounding the assassination of Gedaliah, the first governor of Judah after the Exile began. Cyrus's decree permitting the return didn't come until 537, some forty-five years after even the last of the exiles arrived and sixty-one years after the first came (see the sidebar "How Long Was the Exile?"). During those decades, many of the original deportees would have died, leaving behind descendants born in captivity. Only those who were youths or young adults at the time of the deportation would have still been around, and some of those did return. Ezra 3:12 tells us that when the foundation was laid for the new Temple, those "*older* priests and Levites and heads of families, who had seen the first house, wept aloud when they saw the foundation of this house" (italics added for emphasis).

The Book of Ezra does not describe the 900-mile journey between Babylonia and Judah, but given that Babylonia covered part of modern-day Iraq and that there is significant desert land between there and Judah, it couldn't have been an easy trip. Nonetheless, the group eventually arrived in Jerusalem (2:68) and from there dispersed to the Judean towns from which they or their ancestors had come (2:70).

About the Christian Faith

Through Our Offerings

Often in church, we're invited to participate in special offerings for church-related endeavors in places where we ourselves cannot go. Indeed, even portions of our regular offerings are sometimes channeled through our denomination to support church workers on the other side of the globe. The Book of Ezra shows us there is good precedent for such giving, where those Jews who remained in Babylonia supported those who made the journey to Judah.

Establishing the Altar (Ezra 3)

Not long after arrival in Judah, the "returnees," of their own volition, gathered in Jerusalem to witness the establishment of an altar on the foundations of the original Temple altar, "so that they might offer entirely burned offerings upon it as prescribed in the Instruction from Moses the man of God" (3:2). Those rebuilding the altar worked under the supervision of the priest Jeshua, who was a descendant of the last high priest before the Exile, and Zerubbabel, who, like Sheshbazzar, was a descendant of King David. It's possible that Sheshbazzar and Zerubbabel were the same person, but it's more probable that Zerubbabel was Sheshbazzar's nephew, who succeeded him as governor of Judah.

With the sacrificial system in place, the people went on to celebrate the Festival of Booths, a fall harvest festival that commemorated the time Israel lived in temporary shelters ("booths") during the wilderness period. About seven months later, the leaders of the former exiles commissioned masons and carpenters to begin rebuilding the Temple. The workers soon had the foundation in place, and a dedication service was held. The event brought tears to the eyes of the old-timers who had seen the first Temple and shouts of joy to those who hadn't.

Facing Opposition (Ezra 4:1-5)

To understand what happened next, it's necessary to distinguish the formerly exiled Jews from those who never went into exile. The books of Ezra and Nehemiah tend to speak of the first group as if they comprise all that was left of "true" Israel, but the total of those deported—4,600 (Jeremiah 52:30)—is far too small to equal the population of pre-exilic Judah. What's more, both Jeremiah and the author of Second Kings say that the Babylonians left some of the poorest of the Judahites behind "to tend the vineyards and till the land" (Jeremiah 52:16; 2 Kings 25:12).

Centuries earlier, when the Israelites split into two kingdoms after the death of King Solomon (1 Kings 12), ten tribes stayed with the Northern Kingdom, which retained the name *Israel*, while only the tribes of Judah and Benjamin formed the Southern Kingdom, known as *Judah*. More than 135 years before Judah fell to the Babylonians, the Northern Kingdom was conquered by the Assyrians, who forcibly resettled it with other peoples. In time, these peoples mingled and intermarried with some of the northern Israelites left behind. During the Exile, with many owners of prime real estate in Judah ripped out of the land, those Judahites left behind, along with Israelites and mixed groups from the North, had ensconced themselves into the vacant properties. Intermingled with Israelites, some of these other peoples had begun to worship Israel's God but had continued to worship their own gods as well, a practice abhorrent to the "pure" post-exilic group. (Apparently some of Jews who did not go into exile, and possibly even some of the others, eventually joined the returned group; they did so by "separating themselves from the pollutions of the nations of the land to worship the LORD, the God of Israel" [Ezra 6:21].)

Naturally, when descendants of the Judean property owners returned, there was tension between them and those squatting on the land, but the Ezra account does not address that directly. It mentions, however, that the former exiles were "afraid of the neighboring peoples" (3:3). And, as subsequent events suggest, these neighboring peoples were worried about the former exiles who were reestablishing their place in the land by building a temple.

The writer of Ezra calls these neighboring peoples "enemies of Judah and Benjamin" (4:1). They approached Zerubbabel and the family heads with a seemingly innocent request: "Let's build with you, for we worship your God as you do, and we've been sacrificing to him ever since the days of Assyria's King Esarhaddon, who brought us here" (4:2). The former exiles immediately rejected this, insisting that only they had the exclusive right, by command of both God and King Cyrus, to build the Temple.

Nonetheless, the "enemies" somehow made the former exiles afraid to continue, bringing the work on the Temple to a halt for ten years.

The Temple Completed (Ezra 4:24–6:22)

The material that comes next, 4:6-23, is out of chronological order and concerns later events; we will deal with it in another chapter. The story of the Temple-building resumes at 4:24, reporting again that work on the Temple had stopped because of the opposition and did not resume until the second year of the reign of Persian king Darius.

What got the project moving again was the preaching of two prophets, Haggai and Zechariah (5:1), whose prophecies appear in the two biblical books bearing their names. While reviewing their words is beyond the scope of this study, it's notable that unlike some of the other prophets, these two saw great response to their prophecy. Their preaching effectively jumpstarted the stalled work.

At this point, a second Persian king, Darius, lent his support to the Temple project. His involvement came about when Tattenai, one of the empire's officials in the region including Judah, saw the Temple work underway and inquired who had authorized it. Upon being told that Cyrus had done so, Tattenai wrote to Darius, asking to have the royal archives searched to see if Cyrus actually had issued such a proclamation. It does not appear that Tattenai opposed the Jews; he was simply doing his job, being the "eyes" of the king in this far corner of the empire. Receiving the letter, Darius ordered the archives checked, was shown the memorandum of Cyrus's edict, and wrote back instructing Tattenai not only to allow the work on the Temple to continue, but to pay for it from "royal revenue that is made up of the tribute of the province . . ." and supply the necessary animals and produce for sacrifices (6:8-9).

Thus, in 516 B.C., the Temple was finished and dedicated. The next month, the members of the restored community gathered again to observe Passover. Both the dedication and the Passover were celebrated "joyfully" (6:16, 22), the narrator says, "because the LORD had made them joyful by changing the attitude of the king of Assyria toward them so that he assisted them in the work on the house of God, the God of Israel." Despite the designation *king of Assyria*, this comment probably refers to either Cyrus or Darius. Both were kings of Persia, but Persia had absorbed Babylonia, which had absorbed Assyria, so in truth, the Persian rulers also reigned over Assyria.

In any case, the people of Judah owed a great debt of thanks to these two foreign kings, neither of whom worshiped Israel's God.

Live the Story

The help that two pagan kings, Cyrus and Darius, gave to the Jews to enable them to worship as they chose reminds us that secular governments are often stronger supporters of religious freedom for all than are theocratic ones, which often support one faith to the exclusion of others.

Recognizing the help of Cyrus and Darius for the Jews also reminds us that often, people who don't worship as we do may nonetheless be bearers of comfort, aid, understanding, and tolerance, and may be doers of good deeds.

Where in your life today might you be helped by recognizing that God's purposes are not stymied simply because no person of faith is in a position to change things?

About the Scripture

Ezra-Nehemiah-Esther Chronology

Year(s)	Event	Reference	Persian King
539 B.C.	Capture of Babylonia by the Persians. Persian rule begins.	Daniel 5:30-31	Cyrus (559–530 B.C.)
538–537	Persian king Cyrus's. first year as ruler over the Babylonians and their collapsed empire.	2 Chronicles 36:22; Ezra 1:1-4	
537	First group of Jewish exiles return to Judah	Ezra 1:11	
537	An altar is built on site of the destroyed Jerusalem Temple. Burnt offerings presented. Festival of Booths observed.	Ezra 3:1-6	
536	Work on Temple begun.	Ezra 3:8-10	
536–530	Returnees' enemies oppose Temple construction.	Ezra 4:1-5	
530–520	No work done on Temple, which sits unfinished.	Ezra 4:24	Cambyses II (530–522)[1] Bardiya (522–521)[2]
520	Haggai and Zechariah prophesy. Work on Temple resumes with support of King Darius.	Ezra 5:1-2; 6:14; Haggai 1:14-15; Zechariah 4:6-10	Darius I (521–486)

Year(s)	Event	Reference	Persian King
516	Temple completed.	Ezra 6:14-15	Darius I (521–486)
486	Opponents compose an indictment against the post-exilic community.	Ezra 4:6	Xerxes I (Ahasuerus) (486–465)
483–474	Historical time period for the fictional story of Esther.	Esther 1:1-3	
465	Rebuilding of Jerusalem's walls underway. Opponents send a letter to the king charging that Judahites are planning not to pay tribute once Jerusalem is rebuilt. King suspends the rebuilding.	Ezra 4:7-23	Artaxerxes I (465–424)
about 460[3]	Malachi prophesies in Judah.	Malachi 1:1	
458[4]	Ezra leaves Babylonia and comes to Jerusalem.	Ezra 7:6-9	
458–457	Ezra calls for Jews married to foreign women to separate from them.	Ezra 10:1-44	
445	Twentieth year of King Artaxerxes I.	Nehemiah 1:1	

Year(s)	Event	Reference	Persian King
445	Nehemiah receives permission from Artaxerxes I to go to Jerusalem to rebuild it. Nehemiah leads Jews in reconstruction of the city wall, which is completed in fifty-two days.	Nehemiah 2:1–3:32; 6:15	Artaxerxes I (465–424)
Possibly 445[5]	Ezra assembles the people, reads to them the scroll of Moses. Feast of Booths celebrated. The people fast.	Nehemiah 7:73–8:1; 8:13–9:1	
433–432	Thirty-second year of Artaxerxes I. Nehemiah returns to Babylonia, then comes back to Jerusalem.	Nehemiah 5:14; 13:6-7	

[1] Cambyses II is not mentioned in Ezra or Nehemiah.

[2] Bardiya is not mentioned in Ezra or Nehemiah.

[3] Although Malachi is not mentioned in the books of Ezra and Nehemiah, he most likely prophesied in Judah during this time. His work assumes a functioning Temple and mentions a governor (Malachi 1:8). Also, in Malachi 2:11, he is probably referring to mixed marriages, which was also a concern of Ezra and Nehemiah.

[4] It's possible that some events in the books of Ezra and Nehemiah are out of order. Ezra (the man) was sent by one of the Persian kings named Artaxerxes to perform special assignments. If the king who sent him was Artaxerxes I, then his arrival in Jerusalem was in 458 B.C. If it was Artaxerxes II (who ruled Persia 404–358 B.C.), then Ezra's arrival was in 398 B.C. See Ezra 7:7-8.

[5] Depending on whether Ezra was sent by Artaxerxes I or II (see note 4), these events could belong here in Nehemiah or, as some scholars suggest, either between Ezra 8 and 9 or after Ezra 10.

2.

Embodying God's Law

Ezra 4:6-23; 7:1–10:44

Claim Your Story

The fact that you're reading this book or are part of a group that's using this book as a study guide probably indicates that you're interested in knowing more about what's in the Bible. If that's the case, you're in good company, because Christians have long recognized that knowing what the Bible actually says about God and God's will is vital guidance for how we should live as disciples of Jesus.

What's more, if you happen to be the person leading your study group, or if you teach a Sunday school class or lead some other Bible-learning program, you are helping the church with one of its primary functions: teaching others what the Bible says so that they may embody its precepts in their lives.

I am a minister, and someone once described one of my main roles as being a *"proclaimer* of the Word." That's true, but along the way, I've also realized that equally important roles for me are as *"ascertainer* of the Word" (that is, studying it to know what it says), *"explainer* of the Word" (teaching it to others), and *"framer* of the Word" (trying to live so that I embody it within the boundaries of my life).

Those words—*proclaim, ascertain, explain,* and *frame*—reflect one of the lessons Ezra 7–10 can teach: that as people of faith, we should study God's law, teach and preach it to others, and let it blossom in our lives. That's not to say that every Christian should be a teacher or preacher, for we recognize that those abilities are specific gifts God gives only to some. But all of us should take the time to ascertain—study—what the Word of

God actually says, and then do our best to frame it with our being—put its precepts into practice in our daily lives.

How much time do you put into learning God's Word? How much energy do you put into living its teachings? Are you satisfied with your efforts to learn and live the Bible? Why or why not?

Enter the Bible Story

False Charges Halt Work on Jerusalem (Ezra 4:6-23)

In the previous chapter, we noted that Ezra 4:6-23 was out of chronological order. The content of those verses belongs to the time between Ezra Chapter 6 and Chapter 7. Chapter 6 ends with the completion and dedication of the Temple in Jerusalem during the reign of Persia's king Darius I. When Chapter 7 opens, it is fifty-eight years later, and King Artaxerxes I is ruling Persia's empire. In between these two monarchs, Xerxes I, known in the Bible by his Persian name *Ahasuerus*, sat on Persia's throne. We will hear more about him when we come to the Book of Esther, but he appears in Ezra only in 4:6 and not at all in Nehemiah. Ezra 4:6 says that at the beginning of his rule (486 B.C.), some opponents of the restored community of Jews in Judah composed an indictment about them. The Bible doesn't tell us whether they ever sent it to Ahasuerus or, if they did, whether he did anything about it.

We also don't know the content of that indictment, but it was likely similar in tone at least to a letter later sent by some opponents to King Artaxerxes (4:7-8). The content of that letter appears in 4:9-16 and the king's reply in 4:17-22. The gist of the letter is a charge that the restored community is "rebuilding the rebellious and wicked city [of Jerusalem]...completing the walls and repairing the foundations" (4:12) and that when finished these Jews will refuse to pay tribute to Persia. The alleged planned refusal was a false charge, but Artaxerxes, taking no chances, ordered that the rebuilding of the city stop until he decreed its resumption.

Ironically, this reference to repairing the city's foundations and rebuilding the city walls is the first mention of this activity, and it comes from the Judahites' enemies. In any case, King Artaxerxes' command stopped the work in its tracks, and it would not resume until Nehemiah arrived.

Ezra: Priest and Scribe (Ezra 7:1-10)

Chapter 7 introduces Ezra, a Jew born in Babylonia who was both a priest (7:11) and "a scribe skilled in the Instruction from Moses" (7:6), meaning that he was knowledgeable about and could teach from the Pentateuch, the first five books of the Bible. He also embodied the teachings in his own life.

Not all priests were scribes and not all scribes were priests, but Ezra was both. The priesthood was limited to men from the tribe of Levi, and Ezra was a Levite who could trace his lineage all the way back to Aaron, the first high priest of Israel (7:1-5). In that role, Ezra was ordained to offer sacrifices to God on behalf of the people. As a scribe, Ezra also did religious work, possibly copying and preserving religious documents, but certainly studying them: He was "a scholar of the text of the LORD's commandments and his requirements for Israel" (7:11). One of the books of the Apocrypha describes how scribes burrowed into the texts: "They will seek out the wisdom of all the ancestors, / and they will be occupied with prophecies. / They will preserve the stories of famous people, / and they will penetrate the subtle turns of parables. / They will seek out the hidden meanings of proverbs, / and will live with the puzzles of parables" (Sirach 39:1-3).

Because of their ability to read and write—something that many people in that age could not do—scribes were sometimes also employed by governments to write and copy official documents. It's possible that Ezra did such work for King Artaxerxes, which may be why, when Ezra approached him for help in taking a delegation to Judah, "the king gave him everything he requested" (7:6). Ezra wanted to make this trip because he felt called to "teach law and justice in Israel" (7:10; that is, to the remnant of Israel, the Jews in Judah). There were still many Jews in Babylonia who could be taught as well, but since most of the scribal families had been forced into exile, and because their descendants often took up the same work, there were plenty of scribes in Babylonia to teach the Jews there. Ezra's calling was to teach back in the homeland. There were already priests in Judah—4,289 of them went to Judah with the first group of returnees (Ezra 2:36-39)—so Ezra wasn't needed there in that capacity. But it does not appear there were any scribes, so under the circumstances, when Ezra set out for Judah, it was akin to heading for a mission field.

The Journey to Judah (Ezra 7:11–8:36)

Despite his decision to halt work on Jerusalem's city walls, King Artaxerxes I ultimately did as much good for the post-exilic community as did Cyrus and Darius I before him. He not only granted Ezra and his delegation permission to make the trip to Judah, but he also sent with them a letter (7:11-26) authorizing Ezra to lead a religious reform among the Jews. In fact, he gave Ezra the authority to name "supervisors and judges to adjudicate among all the people in the province Beyond the River who know the laws of your God . . . [and] those [Jews] who do not know them" (7:25). "Beyond the River" was the name of a large administrative area of the Persian Empire of which Judah was a small part. The province lay west of the Euphrates River and included much of what today is Syria and Israel. Thus, the land over which Ezra's appointees would work was very large, but their work was to be only with Jews in those areas. In addition, Artaxerxes authorized Ezra to draw funds from both the royal treasury and the empire treasuries in Beyond the River.

No doubt Ezra expressed gratitude to the king, but the scribe had no doubt who was really behind the king's actions: "Bless the LORD, the God of our ancestors, who has moved the king to glorify the LORD's house in Jerusalem" (7:27).

Ezra 8:1-20 lists the male members of the families that comprised Ezra's delegation, which totaled 1,754. With women and children, the group probably numbered 5,000–6,000. Ezra gathered these people "by the river that runs to Ahava" (8:15) for a three-day fast to ask God for a safe journey. This was no small matter. Ezra had the king's letter, which instructed Persian officials and legions along the way to assist the expedition, but that was no guarantee that all these functionaries would do so wholeheartedly. What's more, there was possible jeopardy from natural calamities, illness, and bandits, and these dangers were compounded by the fact that the group included women and children, as well as large amounts of treasure. Ezra could have requested a bodyguard from the king, but he was "ashamed" (8:22) to do so because the group leaders had told the king that their God was with them, and Ezra didn't want it to appear as if they did not believe that.

The fasting done, the expedition headed toward Judah, 900 miles away. "The power of our God was with us," Ezra said. "He saved us from the power of the enemy and ambushes along the way" (8:31). It's not clear from that wording whether that meant they had no trouble with enemies or whether they were ambushed and God delivered them, but in any case, they arrived intact. Upon arrival, they deposited the silver, gold, and Temple items they had brought with them, participated in worship and made burnt offerings to God, and delivered the king's instructions to the administrators of the province Beyond the River.

Across the Testaments

Marriage to Unbelievers

While Ezra's community looked at the situation of Jews married to Gentiles and decided that separation was the necessary solution, the New Testament church, when faced with a similar situation, came to a different conclusion. In his first letter to the Corinthians, the apostle Paul, as one voice of that church, addressed the matter of Christians married to non-Christians. He wrote,

> If a believer has a wife who doesn't believe, and she agrees to live with him, then he shouldn't divorce her. If a woman has a husband who doesn't believe and he agrees to live with her, then she shouldn't divorce him. The husband who doesn't believe belongs to God because of his wife, and the wife who doesn't believe belongs to God because of her husband. Otherwise your children would be contaminated by the world, but now they are spiritually set apart. But if a spouse who doesn't believe chooses to leave, then let them leave. The brother or sister isn't tied down in these circumstances. God has called you to peace. How do you know as a wife if you will save your husband? Or how do you know as a husband if you will save your wife? (1 Corinthians 7:12-16)

The Communal Problem (Ezra 9:1–10:44)

Not long after Ezra and his entourage arrived in Judah, he learned that some of the Jewish men who had returned to Judah in previous migrations, or had been born to those returnees, had intermarried with women from other national groups in the area, groups that had practices "detestable" (9:1) to the Jews. Almost certainly those practices involved idol worship and non-kosher diets, but there were probably lifestyle issues that faithful Jews would eschew as well. Beyond these issues, however, was the more basic fact that over the centuries, Israel's prophets and teachers had taught the Hebrews that they were chosen by God to be God's own. They were called to be a *holy* nation, which meant not only righteous, but *separated*, dedicated for God's own purposes. The marital unions with Gentile women who worshiped other gods increased the likelihood of apostasy on the part of the Jewish community. But intermarriages were also viewed as the pollution of the chosen people, those who were called to keep themselves apart from the general stream of humankind in specific ways so that their testimony and practices would be a witness to the nations of the one true God.

The Jews in these mixed marriages included some from all segments of the community—priests and Levites, as well as laity. (Although the text deals only with Jewish men married to Gentile women, 9:12 implies that some Jewish women had married Gentile men.) Ezra immediately understood these mixed marriages as acts of "unfaithfulness" (9:2) to God, both by the men who had entered into them and by the Jewish community that had tolerated them. No doubt Ezra based this conclusion on such passages as Deuteronomy 7:3-4: "Don't intermarry with [other peoples]. Don't give your daughter to one of their sons to marry, and don't take one of their daughters to marry your son, because they will turn your child away from following me so that they end up serving other gods. That will make the LORD's anger burn against you, and he will quickly annihilate you" (see also Exodus 34:11-16). To be clear, Ezra's concern was not racial or ethnic mixing but about danger from apostasy.

Ezra believed this unfaithfulness was likely to bring God's judgment on the community. He immediately went into a penitential mode, falling on his knees before God and praying a prayer in which he acknowledged "*our* iniquities" (Ezra 9:6, italics added), including himself in the sinful community. He viewed the release from the Exile as something of a last chance for the people of Israel. Many Israelites had already been absorbed into other cultures, and he didn't want the remaining "pure" ones to "blow it" by discarding their covenantal relationship with God. Thus he prayed, "But now, for *a brief while* the LORD our God has shown favor in leaving us survivors and in giving us a stake in his holy place" (9:8, italics added). They had a window of opportunity, Ezra decided, but it could soon close due to the community's unfaithfulness.

As Ezra prayed, members of the community gathered around him and "wept in distress" (10:1). Eventually, one of the men, Shecaniah, proposed to Ezra that those men who had married non-Jewish women send their wives away, along with any children born to those unions. Ezra agreed and got the people to make a "solemn pledge" (10:5) that they would do this. Ezra then chose a committee of "certain men, heads of families" (10:16) to oversee the execution of this pledge. This committee eventually determined that 110 men had married women from the neighboring peoples. Ezra 10:18-43 lists the names of these 110 men. In the Common English Bible rendering of Ezra 10:44, it says, "All these men had married foreign women, some of whom had borne children," but gives no resolution. However, a footnote on that verse acknowledges that the underlying Hebrew is "uncertain," and notes that the parallel verse in First Esdras in the Apocrypha says, "They sent them away with their children" (1 Esdras 9:36). The New Revised Standard Version translates Ezra 10:44 as, "All these had married foreign women, and they sent them away with their children."

This is a difficult story for modern readers, for from what we now understand of God's love for the world (see John 3:16), it is hard to imagine that God would have wanted these men to divorce their Gentile wives and turn their children away. Divorce and broken families are hard enough in our day, but they created even greater hardships back then. In those cultures, women had little opportunity to earn a living and were dependent on their husbands for support. Breaking up these families would have caused economic privation for the women and children, as well as personal misery and broken hearts for all parties concerned.

Perhaps the best we can do is to try to understand the mindset of Ezra's community, where being "chosen" and needing to stay "separated" had been drummed into them since birth. We should also note that the threat from idolatry was very real. No less an important Israelite than their ancestor King Solomon had eventually turned to the worship of other gods after marrying several foreign women who brought their idols into his palace with them.

Live the Story

Few of us today would embrace the rupturing of existing, functional families as an appropriate act of faithfulness to God. We may even question whether it was the right thing in Ezra's day. Nonetheless, we can recognize where Ezra's community got it right: They concluded that since they had strayed far from their covenant relationship with God, radical changes were necessary to show their desire for God to restore them. Even today, when we have turned away from God and wish to "come home" spiritually, isn't it important that we stop doing the things that draw us away from God? And in some cases, maybe we need to take some radical steps to make our change of direction possible.

None of that is to suggest that we "earn" our own salvation by straightening out our lives. Salvation comes from God, not us. But many times, there are hindrances we can remove. We can come up with a "rip-out list" to open the way for righteousness to take root. Do we have friends who nudge us away from God? Maybe we need to spend less time with them. Are we toying with temptation to marital unfaithfulness with someone at work? Perhaps we need to request a transfer to another department. Does our attachment to possessions get in the way of loving our neighbor as we love ourselves? Maybe we need to give away more of what we own.

A right relationship with God is *that* important.

When we recognize that we can learn even from Bible stories like this one, we can frame its underlying principles in our lives and, under the proper circumstances, teach them to others. Rather than being a book of ancient history, the Bible becomes a living document, one that helps us navigate the shoals of daily life.

In the "Claim the Story" section that opens this session, we asked three questions: How much time do you put into learning God's Word? How much energy do you put into living its teachings? Are you satisfied with your efforts to learn and live the Bible? Following your answers to those three, it's time now for two more: What would you have to change to do these things more fully? Which of those changes are you willing to make?

3.

Dealing With Opposition

Nehemiah 1:1–7:73a

Claim Your Story

While I was attending seminary, I also served as student pastor of a small rural church. One day a young-adult member—let's call him Ken—came to me with an idea. There were many teenagers in the community, but in our rural location, there wasn't much for them to do. Ken, who had grown up in that congregation and attended regularly, proposed that our church organize a youth center to be open on Friday evenings in the nearby town hall building. He had in mind a kind of gathering place with live music and refreshments, where teenagers could hang out in a wholesome environment supervised by church members who had volunteered to help.

Ken had already done an impressive bit of investigation—he had learned what was necessary to secure use of the town hall, checked on getting vending machines for food and drink, looked into local bands, and talked to the county sheriff about security—so I was quick to support his project. The next step, I said, was to present the idea to the congregation, so I put it on the agenda for the next church council meeting. In the meantime, Ken explained his idea informally to several people in the church.

When the night of the meeting came, one member, the father of a teenaged girl who would potentially attend the youth center, surprised all of us by speaking vehemently against the proposal. While not exactly attacking Ken's motives or mine, he nonetheless raged against the plan, painting problem scenarios so farfetched as to suggest that the idea of the youth center itself was evil. It was also clear that he was absolutely intent on killing it. No other member of the council seemed as opposed as this man did, but none spoke in favor of the plan either, and without the council's support, we couldn't proceed. The youth center never happened.

As a relative newcomer in the community, I had no idea where this otherwise mild-mannered church member's venom had come from, and neither did other church members who had known him for years. I have since wondered if he had been victimized as a teenager at some similar center and was carrying the emotional scars. But whatever the reason, he stopped what might have been a good outreach ministry of that church in its tracks.

Have you ever faced resolute opposition when trying to do what you perceived as the Lord's work? Have you been blindsided in a ministry effort by someone from within the church? How about from someone outside the church? Can such tough resistance mean you were mistaken in assuming that your endeavor was God's will? How can you know? How should you respond to opposition when you are convinced what you are attempting is God's will?

The story of Nehemiah helps us think through such questions.

Enter the Bible Story

The Man, the Time, and the Place (Nehemiah 1:1-3)

The Book of Nehemiah opens by identifying the writer: "Nehemiah, Hacaliah's son"; the time: "the month of Kislev, in the twentieth year"; the place: "the fortress city of Susa"; and the circumstance: "Those in the province who survived the captivity are in great trouble and shame" (Nehemiah 1:1, 3).

Nehemiah was a Jew born in Babylonia, which by then was incorporated into the Persian Empire. Beyond the name of his father, we know nothing about his background. Susa was an important city in the empire, and when Persian king Artaxerxes I was in residence there, Nehemiah was his cupbearer (1:11b), a kind of wine steward. In that role, Nehemiah not only served the king his wine—which put him in frequent and close proximity to the king—but also tasted it first to ensure that it was not poisoned. Only someone who had the king's implicit trust would serve in this position.

The "twentieth year" refers to Artaxerxes' reign; he was in his twentieth year as monarch. Since he ruled from 465 to 424 B.C., that means Nehemiah's story begins in 445 B.C. The month, Kislev, is not particularly important to the story, but it does reflect something about the exile period that first brought large groups of Jews to Babylonia (see Session 1, "How Long Was the Exile?"). *Kislev* is the name for the ninth month on the Hebrew calendar, but it was derived from the Old Babylonian month name *Kissilimu*. Rabbinic tradition says Babylonian month names were introduced into the Jewish calendar by returnees from the Exile. That the Jews adopted a Babylonian month name suggests how deeply they were marked by their time in captivity.

The first group of released Jewish exiles had returned to Judah in 537 B.C., ninety-two years before Nehemiah's story begins; but those nine decades had not been an easy time in the Jewish homeland. Though the people had reestablished themselves in Judah and had rebuilt the Temple, it was still a time of "trouble and shame." Nearly a century after their return, Jerusalem's walls, which had been torn down by the Babylonians in 586 B.C., still hadn't been rebuilt. A start had been made about 465 B.C., but after false charges by opponents of the restored community, Artaxerxes had ordered the work stopped (see Ezra 4:23), which was enforced by the royal deputy Rehum. It's possible that Rehum not only halted the work but had what had been rebuilt to that point torn down as well.

As far as we know, Nehemiah himself had never been to Jerusalem or anywhere else in Judah, but his brother Hanani had (1:2), and he brought a report to Nehemiah of conditions in their ancestral city. This news grieved Nehemiah. He had never seen Jerusalem, but with it being the seat of the Davidic kings of Israel and with the Temple located there, it was the geographic center of his ethnic- and faith-identity.

The Project Conceived, Authorized, and Funded (Nehemiah 1:4–2:8)

Nehemiah's grief moved him to fast and pray "night and day" (1:6). Nehemiah 1:5-11 contains one of Nehemiah's prayers in which he addressed God as one who "keeps covenant" (1:5), which refers to the promise God made to Israel through Abraham and renewed under Moses to be Israel's God. But Nehemiah was aware that covenant-keeping required faithfulness from both parties, so he acknowledged that the people of Israel, including himself and his family, needed God's forgiveness for failing to keep the commandments. He asked God to help his people and give success to a plan that Nehemiah had conceived.

That plan involved Nehemiah taking advantage of his access to the Persian king. He wanted to act personally to help Jerusalem, and only the king could provide him the authorization and the means to do so. But to approach the emperor on this matter was not without risk: Artaxerxes' own order had halted the work on the walls twenty years previously (Ezra 4:21-23). What's more, court protocol dictated that one did not burden the monarch with one's own problems unless invited by the king to do so. The king had absolute power, and if he felt imposed upon, he could have the offender banished or even executed. Thus, Nehemiah proceeded prudently. Rather than broach the matter directly, he allowed his sadness to show on his face, which led the king to inquire as to its source. This was the moment when everything Nehemiah hoped to accomplish could founder and his very existence could be ended. Thus Nehemiah reported, "I was very afraid" (2:2b). But we can almost hear him take a deep breath and press on, saying to the king, "May the king live forever! Why shouldn't I seem sad when the city, the place of my family's graves, is in ruins and its gates destroyed by fire?" (2:3).

At that, the king responded, "What is it that you need?" (2:4).

Nehemiah requested that he be sent to Judah, "that I may rebuild it" (2:5). Artaxerxes not only agreed, but he also issued the necessary permissions for the journey across the empire and directives for building supplies. He even appointed Nehemiah governor of Judah (5:14).

Just as a century earlier, when Persian king Cyrus permitted the exiles to go home and equipped them for the journey, Persian king Artaxerxes now permitted the rebuilding of Jerusalem and equipped Nehemiah for the task. But we should not overlook the activity of God behind the scenes. The critical juncture in the conversation between Nehemiah and Artaxerxes occurred when the latter responded, "What is it that you need?" for he could as easily have said, "Get out of my sight!" Surely Nehemiah saw the king's favorable question as evidence that his prayers had been answered. He said as much in 2:8b: "The king gave me what I asked, *for the gracious power of my God was with me*" (italics added).

The Project Launched (Nehemiah 2:9–3:32)

Armed with letters of safe passage from the king, Nehemiah set out for Jerusalem accompanied by "officers of the [Persian] army and cavalry" (2:9). It was probably good that Nehemiah had the military escort, for some of the officials to whom the letters were addressed were none too happy about his mission. Two officials especially, Sanballat and Tobiah, were "angry that someone had come to seek the welfare of the people of Israel" (2:10). The former was governor of Samaria, the district immediately north of Judah. He may also have been the caretaker official in charge of Judah until a new governor was appointed. If that was the case, then Nehemiah was displacing him from that role. Tobiah is identified as "the Ammonite," which may have meant he was the governor of Ammon, the district east of Judah across the Jordan River, but he may just as likely have been a sub-official under Sanballat. Whatever their objections, Nehemiah carried on without interruption.

Nehemiah made his first move on the third night after arrival. Taking just a few people with him, he made an inspection of the remains of the city walls. While we can assume the night was moonlit enough to make such a tour feasible, it's likely Nehemiah chose to look things over at night to avoid alerting those like Sanballat and Tobiah who opposed rebuilding the walls. Nehemiah was mounted on an animal as he circled the old city, but at one point he had to dismount and proceed on foot because of obstructing rubble, which suggests that the destruction was extensive.

Soon thereafter, Nehemiah called together the Jewish community and told them his plan to rebuild the wall, adding that God had commissioned him and that the Persian king supported the project. "Come, let's rebuild the wall of Jerusalem," he said, "so that we won't continue to be in disgrace" (2:17). He was not speaking of their reputation as a people, however, but of God's reputation among non-Israelites who saw the sorry state of Jerusalem and concluded that Judah's God was not strong enough to help them. By rebuilding, Nehemiah intended not only to aid his fellow Jews, but also to rehabilitate God's reputation. The people immediately agreed to support Nehemiah's plan.

When Chapter 3 opens, the wall project is underway. The whole chapter is a listing of those who worked on the project, naming individuals, families, and community groups and the segments of the wall that each team rebuilt. Of significance is that the workers came not just from Jerusalem itself, but from towns throughout Judah. There were groups from Jericho (3:2), Tekoa (3:5, 27) Gibeon and Mizpah (3:7), and Zanoah (3:13), as well as from several larger administrative districts of Judah. It must have thrilled those who had ancestral holdings in Jerusalem itself to see their fellow Judahites laboring on the walls with them. But even those who had no personal land claims within the city boundaries had a stake in the project, for Jerusalem was the center of their identity as people in covenant with the Lord.

Dealing With Opposition and a Communal Problem (Nehemiah 4–6)

As the word of the project spread, opposition quickly appeared from Sanballat and Tobiah, now in company with Geshem, an Arab leader. These men mocked Nehemiah's plan and accused him of rebelling against the king. Nehemiah responded, "The God of heaven will give us success," and told the trio they "will have no share, right, or claim in Jerusalem" (2:20).

After the interruption of the list of wall workers in Chapter 3, Chapter 4 resumes the story of the opposition from Sanballat and his cronies, which soon moved beyond mere words to an actual plot to attack the wall crews (4:8), probably with a band of thugs. Nehemiah learned of this plot, however, and stationed guards around the workers, eventually splitting his crews so that one half guarded while the other half worked, and even those who worked kept weapons within reach. The sight of the armed workers and guards apparently was sufficient, for no attack came. Nehemiah acted prudently, but he credited the Lord, saying God had "spoiled" the opponents' plot (4:15). At no point did Nehemiah allow the work to stop.

While the work continued, Nehemiah had to deal with an obstacle to community life from within the community itself. Many of the poorer members had had to mortgage their fields and houses to wealthy members both to purchase food and to pay the king's tax. The interest rate charged by lenders had forced many of the poor to the point where the only option they had left was to indenture their sons and daughters to the lenders. These debtors complained to Nehemiah because they were being victimized by people of their "same flesh and blood" (5:5).

This news angered Nehemiah, for exacting interest from fellow Israelites was forbidden by Mosaic law (see Exodus 22:25-27), was detrimental to the community itself, and exposed God's people to the taunts of their enemies. He called the people together and blasted them, saying, "To the best of our ability. . . we have bought back our Jewish kin who had been sold to other nations. But now you are selling your own kin, who must then be bought back by us!" (5:8). Such was the respect Nehemiah commanded that the lenders agreed without argument to return properties taken as collateral and stop charging interest to fellow Judahites.

In 5:14-19, Nehemiah explained that although he was entitled to extract a "governor's food allowance" from the people he governed, he did not take it because he was "God-fearing" (5:15) and did not want to lay that burden on his people. In fact, he regularly fed a large number of people at his table, at his own expense.

Chapter 6 details more efforts by Sanballat and cohorts to derail the wall construction, including inviting Nehemiah to a "meeting" in a distant town where he would not be protected by his people, sending him letters in which they accused him of plotting to proclaim himself king and threatening to make that charge known to the emperor, and paying the prophet Shemaiah to convince Nehemiah to go into hiding to save himself from a supposed assassination attempt. In each case, however,

Nehemiah saw through the ruses and remained steadfastly on the wall project, which was completed in just fifty-two days (6:15).

Nehemiah reported that the finished wall made the surrounding nations "afraid," and he declared, "They knew that this work was completed with the help of our God" (6:16).

Finishing the wall did not bring an end to the opposition. Nehemiah 6:17-19 tells of correspondence between Tobiah and some nobles of Judah who had allegiance to him. These nobles touted to Nehemiah Tobiah's supposed good deeds (probably political favors to them) and reported back to Tobiah what Nehemiah said. Tobiah also sent letters to Nehemiah that were intended to intimidate him. None of this deterred Nehemiah, however.

Almost certainly, the interference of Sanballat, Tobiah, and Geshem was motivated primarily by their desire to hold onto power they had grabbed before Nehemiah's arrival, but that probably wasn't the whole reason. The exclusivist view of the Jewish community itself also may have provoked resistance. The Judahites understood their work not only as building a safe haven for themselves, but also as rebuilding the stronghold

Across the Testaments

Shaking Out the Robes

After Nehemiah confronted the wealthy members of the community about extracting interest when loaning to less well-off members, they promised to stop doing so. Nehemiah then took a symbolic action to seal their promise. He shook out the fold of his robe and said, "So may God shake out everyone from their house and property if they don't keep this promise. So may they be shaken out and emptied!" (5:13). Perhaps the apostle Paul had Nehemiah in mind when, in Corinth, he made a similar gesture against members of the synagogue who argued against him when he testified that Jesus was the Christ. Acts 18:6 says, "When they opposed and slandered him, [Paul] shook the dust from his clothes in protest and said to them, 'You are responsible for your own fates! I'm innocent! From now on I'll go to the Gentiles!'"

of Israel's God. Thus, they didn't welcome participation from people who did not worship Israel's God, who worshiped God along with false gods, or who worshiped God in "non-kosher" ways. And the neighboring peoples likely weren't happy about an organized population nearby whose attitude was "Our God is better than yours" and "We are God's chosen people; you are not" (such is implied in Ezra 4:1-3 and Nehemiah 2:20).

The Project Completed (Nehemiah 7:1-73a)

Once the final gates were hung, closing the last gaps in the wall, Nehemiah appointed gatekeepers and a permanent guard to control access into Jerusalem. With the wall intact and guarded, houses in Jerusalem could now be rebuilt.

The balance of Chapter 7 includes a list of the first returnees from Babylonia, which Nehemiah found while preparing to conduct a census of the restored community of Jews in Judah. The chapter concludes by saying, "The people of Israel were settled in their towns."

Live the Story

Nehemiah never won over his opponents, but he succeeded despite them. In the case of the proposed youth center mentioned earlier, perhaps we could have established it despite the church member who argued so strongly against it. But the fact that no other church members supported the project makes me think that the plan was not a call from God, for one of the ways that we learn whether something is God's will or not is by airing it in the church. If the combined wisdom of a congregation does not support it, then we should at least consider that we may have been mistaken.

Back then, I thought the congregation was simply being obstinate, but perhaps I should have read Nehemiah's story. Nehemiah possessed qualities often needed when facing tough tasks that not everyone supports. He had courage, perseverance, leadership ability, and the wisdom to see though traps and plots against the project. Most of all, though, he had a clear sense that God was behind him, and he was quick to credit God's help and faithfulness.

When we face opposition while attempting what we perceive to be the Lord's work, it's worth considering whether the problems we encounter can be overcome with courage, perseverance, leadership, and wisdom, or whether they are signals from God that we have misunderstood God's will. The answer will not be the same in every case, but if we can determine that God is indeed calling us to a particular work, then we can count on God to help us.

What personal qualities do you bring to your work for the Lord? Which qualities do you need to ask God to strengthen? For which ones do you need to rely on others? For what efforts do you need to seek to know God's will more fully?

4.

Hearing and Doing

Nehemiah 7:73b–13:31

Claim Your Story

As a preacher, there's one sentence of sermon feedback that drives me nuts. That's when someone who has heard my sermon says, "You gave me something to think about." I mean, what's the point of working on a sermon all week if the only thing I accomplish on Sunday is to give people something to think about? You can stay home and read the Sunday paper to find something to think about!

Besides, what's the person actually trying to say? If he or she means, "I don't understand what you told us, but I'm trying to be polite," then I have to take responsibility for not communicating clearly. If the person means, "What you told us is so unexpected that I need some time to mull it over before I can decide what do with it," then I may have accomplished something, but only if the person actually does the mulling over and comes to some kind of active conclusion. If he or she means, "I don't really know what to do with what you told us," then I have to take responsibility for that too, because that means that while I may have communicated my theme clearly and maybe even stirred people up, I failed to tell them what they might do in response. If what the person intends is to say, "I disagree with what you told us, but I'm trying to be polite," I have no problem, because certainly I don't have the final word on how someone should live. But if the person means, "I understand and agree with what you said, but I don't intend to do anything with it," I would be especially unhappy, because if my preaching can't move people to progress in their faith or practice of Christianity, then I'm wasting my time.

What about you? Do you expect to do anything in your life differently as the result of listening to a sermon? Do you allow that, despite whatever human failings the preacher might have, God might, through the preacher's words, nonetheless challenge you to make some change in your life? What about when you attend a Sunday school class, spend time in private prayer, or read the Bible? Do you expect that God might nudge you to change how you act as a result of what you hear from God while engaged in these activities?

To a large degree, questions like these set the stage for understanding the second half of the Book of Nehemiah, for these chapters tell how members of the post-exilic community in Judah heard the word of God and realized that God's words were not just "something to think about," but actually entailed "something to do."

If you are going to read on, beware, for God might speak to you as well.

Enter the Bible Story

One of the contributions of the Common English Bible (CEB) has been to word differently what older Bible versions translated as "the book of the law of Moses." In the CEB, it's regularly translated as "the Instruction scroll from Moses" (as, for example, in Nehemiah 8:1). Both "law" and "Instruction" are reasonable renderings of the underlying Hebrew word *Torah*, but for many twenty-first-century readers, "the Instruction scroll from Moses" conveys better what's intended by *Torah*. We tend to think of *laws* as something designed to warn us away from specific conduct and promise us punishment if we don't obey them. *Instructions*, on the other hand, sound like something designed to help us avoid unnecessary snags and promise us better success if we follow them.

What's more, the "law *of* Moses" may cause some to think of Moses as the originator of the Torah, while "Instruction *from* Moses" makes it easier to understand Moses as the conveyer of *God's* law/instruction, which is, of course, the case. Other verses identify more clearly that the Torah comes from the Lord. Nehemiah 8:18 in the New Revised Standard Version, for example, speaks of "the book of the law of God"; the CEB renders it "God's Instruction scroll."

For centuries, Jews have understood the content of the Torah to be the first five books of the Bible, also referred to as the Pentateuch. But for Jews, these five biblical books are not merely one of the sections of the Hebrew Bible; they are seen as the directions and teaching (thus "instruction") that God gave as *the source of life* for the Jewish people. Thus, as we will see, when some Levites in Nehemiah's day led the people in remembering God's mighty help for their ancestors, they said, "You also warned them to return to your Instruction, / but they acted arrogantly and didn't obey your commands. / They sinned against your judgments, *even though life comes by keeping them*" (Nehemiah 9:29, italics added).

Hearing the Instruction Scroll From Moses (Nehemiah 8)

In the Hebrew Bible, the books of Ezra and Nehemiah were originally a single book called Ezra. It was not separated into two volumes until sometime in the third century after Christ. Many Bible scholars question the placement of Nehemiah 8–10, for chronologically it seems to belong either between Ezra 8 and 9 or after Ezra 10. Additionally, Nehemiah 8–10 seems almost to interrupt the narration flow from Nehemiah 7 to Nehemiah 11. Nonetheless, as an episode in its own right, the action in Nehemiah 8–10 clearly belongs to the whole Ezra-Nehemiah history.

Assuming these three chapters are not misplaced, however, the action flowing from the public reading of the Instruction scroll from Moses occurs just a few days after the completion of the rebuilding of the Jerusalem wall. Nehemiah 6:15 reports that the wall was finished on the "twenty-fifth day of the month of Elul," which was the sixth month on the Hebrew calendar. The public reading of the Instruction scroll from Moses occurred "when the seventh month came" (7:73b). Thus, the excitement of finishing the wall was still in the air.

In that spirit, "all the people gathered together in the area in front of the Water Gate" (8:1), probably so named because it was the nearest access from the city to the spring of Gihon. And there assembled, the people asked Ezra to bring out the Instruction scroll from Moses and read it to them. Clearly, it was the people and not Ezra who initiated the reading, and as the narrative continues, it appears that this was the first time most of them had heard its words. But why? Were these not Jews?

We know from the Bible itself that at least some of the Torah had long been in existence, for during the reign of Judah's king Josiah (640–609 B.C.), a copy of the Instruction scroll was found in the Temple while that structure was being refurbished (2 Kings 22:8). As we noted in Session 2, scribes became scholars of the Lord's commands, and there were numerous scribes among the exiles in Babylonia, so it's likely that the ancestors of the returnees had been taught from the Instruction scroll. But the first return to Judah had occurred ninety-two years before the Jerusalem wall was rebuilt, and, as we also noted in Session 2, there were apparently no scribes among the returnees, which meant the generation that worked on the wall had not themselves heard the words of the Mosaic Instruction. They had likely heard about the scroll, however, from older relatives, and now they wanted to hear its teachings for themselves.

Ezra, who was a scribe as well as a priest, was quick to comply with their request. And so, at a public gathering near the Water Gate, Ezra read the scroll, with help from thirteen Levites who translated it into Aramaic for the people. (This was necessary because the text was in Hebrew, which the ordinary people did not understand.)

The people received this reading of the Instruction scroll seriously, standing up when Ezra first unrolled it. When Ezra blessed the Lord, the people responded with a twofold "amen," which indicated their acceptance of what was being read. As they listened, they must have been struck by how far their daily practices were from the holiness the text called for, and they began weeping. At that point, both Ezra and Nehemiah told them to rejoice instead, because "the joy from the LORD is your strength!" (8:10). In other words, God was calling *them* to be the current community in covenant with him. God was giving *them* the teachings that make for a wholesome and holy life, which is a source of joy. The Instruction from God, written during previous generations, was now the Word of God *to them*. When the people understood this, a "great celebration" (8:12) took place. The Instruction now became the basis of their existence as a community, and their faith and practice were to be dominated by it.

The study of the Instruction scroll continued the next day, though now with only the family heads and religious leaders in attendance. In the reading, they came to the description of the Festival of Booths their ancestors had observed to remember God's care as they wandered in the wilderness after the exodus from Egypt. Learning that this festival was held in the seventh month, these leaders called their fellow Jews to observe it as well. They built "booths"—temporary shelters like those used by their ancestors in the wilderness—and lived in them for seven days, as the Instruction scroll prescribed. And each day, Ezra read more to them from the scroll.

About the Christian Faith

The Bible Is Our Book

Before the members of the post-exilic community actually heard the content of the Instruction scroll from Moses, they had already heard about it. They knew it was the book their ancestors had revered and sought to live by. They also knew it wasn't initially addressed to their generation. But after hearing it read, they embraced it for themselves; it became *their* book, and they were then the community in covenant with God.

In much the same way, the Bible as a whole has become *our* book. When we become Christians, we too enter the community in covenant with God. The Bible is the book of that community, and so its words, though not authored originally for us, have things to say to us. The Bible becomes the Word of God to us.

Thus, when reading the Bible, we can say, "While I know these words were originally written for another time and place, God has chosen to communicate to me through them today."

A Day of Repentance (Nehemiah 9–10)

The words from the Instruction continued to work in the hearts and minds of those who had heard it, so that later in the month, the people observed a day of repentance. This was not a standard festival, but a special observance, perhaps initiated by the common citizenry. The location isn't specified, but it may have been in the Temple, since for that day, all foreigners were excluded. Wherever it was, the Jewish community "stood to confess their sins and the terrible behavior of their ancestors" (9:2). As before, their observance also included more reading from the Instruction scroll, which they did for "a quarter of the day" (9:3). Then, on behalf of the whole assembly, several Levites offered a prayer, which is contained in 9:5b-37. It includes praise of God, a recitation of God's mighty acts in the history of the Israelites, admission of the sins of their ancestors, and recognition that in spite of those sins, God "didn't forsake them" (9:17). The Levites then turned to the condition of the present generation, affirming that God had "acted faithfully" while they had "done wrong" (9:33). They further acknowledged that their current situation as a people under foreign domination was the outcome of the waywardness of their ancestors and of their own sins.

The people then put into writing their intention to live according to their best understanding of the Instruction scroll. They specifically pledged not to intermarry with neighboring peoples, not to conduct business on the Sabbath or any holy day, to observe a Sabbath year every seventh year, to pay the Temple tax, to make the prescribed sacrifices, to dedicate firstborn males to the Lord (their sons were to be ransomed back, however, and not sacrificed [see Exodus 13:13-16]), to tithe the produce of the land, and not to neglect the Temple or its functions. On behalf of the whole community, the leaders (including Nehemiah), priests, and Levites affixed their names on the seal of the document.

While the desire of the people to live by the words of the Instruction scroll is commendable, the parts of it they pulled out to commit themselves to are those related to racial exclusiveness and ceremonial obligations. These were important for their cohesiveness as a subject people under foreign rule, and were among the most visible signs of their uniqueness as the chosen people. The larger themes of the Torah, however, received no mention in the commitment document the people of the postexilic community signed on their day of repentance. Those larger unmentioned themes include the practices and prohibitions encapsulated in the Ten Commandments (Exodus 20:1-17; Deuteronomy 5:1-22), and the teachings about justice (such as Exodus 23:1-9), mercy (such as Exodus 22:26-27), and moral holiness (such as Leviticus 19:9-18), all of which are prominent in the Instruction scroll. We should not assume that they intended to ignore these weightier matters, but we simply note that those to which they committed in writing had to do with maintaining their identity in terms of ethnicity and ritual.

Repopulating Jerusalem, Dedicating the Wall, Restoring the Temple (Nehemiah 11–13)

In reporting the completion of the city wall, Nehemiah 7 included this brief comment: "Now although the city was wide and large, only a few people were living within it, and no houses had been rebuilt" (7:4). This gives some idea of the extent of the destruction the Babylonian army had inflicted on the city back in 586 B.C., but it also tells of the problem facing Nehemiah and the wall-rebuilders: If the city was to be viable, it needed a population. After the interruption of other events, Chapter 11 reports how this matter was resolved. We're not told who made the decision—perhaps Nehemiah or perhaps the community leaders—but it was decided that ten percent of the Jewish population of Judah should live in the city. To accomplish this, the people cast lots to determine which one out of every ten should move inside the city walls. Although today we think of the outcome of such practices as casting of lots to be a matter of chance, in that day, it was thought to be a way of discovering the will of God.

Some people volunteered to live in the city, and the people as a whole blessed those who offered. We don't know if the volunteers were too few or too many, but either way, the casting of lots resolved the matter by designating who should actually live in Jerusalem. It's likely that some of those so selected would have preferred to remain where they were, having already established themselves in an outlying community or living in homes inherited from their ancestors. Nonetheless, there's no mention of anyone refusing to make the move; those selected by lot apparently accepted that it was God's will for them to go. And thus, Jerusalem was repopulated.

The balance of Chapter 11 tells who specifically was selected for the resettlement and gives some information about the distribution of the rest of the people throughout Judah.

Nehemiah 12:1-26 contains listings of priests and Levites from two different periods: first, those who returned from exile with Zerubbabel, and second, those from a generation later. These lists may have been included to show that even though the Temple had not been built, the *work* of the Temple was properly cared for from the time Zerubbabel brought the first group of returnees right down to the time of Ezra and Nehemiah (see 12:26, 47). The rest of the chapter (12:27-47) describes the dedication of the reconstructed city wall, which Nehemiah organized, and the appointment of men to certain Temple responsibilities. (In 12:31, "I" is Nehemiah; see the footnote in the CEB.)

Sometime after the dedication of the wall, Nehemiah returned to Babylonia, within the Persian Empire, where he reported to King Artaxerxes. The king apparently then sent Nehemiah back to Judah for a second term as governor of the province (13:6-7; compare with 5:14). During Nehemiah's absence, one of the Temple priests who was related to Tobiah made available a room at the Temple for his kinsman's use. During that same period, the people in general had become slack in their support of the Levites and had begun conducting business on the Sabbath. What's more, some Jews had married non-Jewish women. So upon Nehemiah's return, he expelled Tobiah from the Temple, scolded the people for their lack of support for the Levites, closed the city gates on the Sabbath so that no commerce could take place, and angrily reminded the people of their pledge not to marry foreigners. Unlike what Ezra had done, however, Nehemiah apparently didn't require those already in such marriages to divorce their spouses.

Nehemiah himself was a strong governor and a faithful keeper of the covenant with God, but it must have been discouraging to him to see how quickly some members of the community became careless about their religious commitments when he wasn't on hand to supervise them.

The book closes with Nehemiah's prayer: "Remember me, my God, for good" (13:31).

Live the Story

As we suggested earlier, when it comes to hearing something from God—perhaps a call for renewed commitment or for reforming some aspect of our lives—it's not sufficient merely to think about those things, although thoughtful consideration and evaluation are necessary, of course. But eventually, once we have concluded that God really has nudged us or even called us more directly, we actually should *do* something positive in response. The members of the post-exilic community illustrate that beautifully when, hearing the Torah read at the Water Gate, they were moved first to repentance and then to reform how they had been living. Admittedly, by the end of the Book of Nehemiah, some had become less than faithful to the commitments they had made, but that reminds us of the importance of taking deliberate steps to stay in frequent touch with God.

What practices do you need to institute in your life to give yourself time to listen for God? What things have you heard that you think may be from God but that you have left in the realm of only thinking about? How can you involve some people from the church in evaluating whether what you are hearing is indeed from God? And once convinced, what do you need to do in response, and when do you plan to do it?

5.

The Diaspora

Esther 1–4

Claim Your Story

Do you know the word *diaspora* (di-AS-po-ra)? Generically, it refers to a dispersion of people from their original homeland. In that meaning, New Orleans had a diaspora following the devastation from the 2005 hurricanes Katrina and Rita. Due to the widespread destruction of homes, places of employment, schools, hospitals, public services, and much of the city's infrastructure, a sizable portion of the population was evacuated to other communities across America, and many of those people have never returned. Jobs in their new locations, lack of funds, or other reasons may keep them from going back, but even so, many still think of themselves as New Orleanians. Even after several years in their new communities, some still feel that they are not at home, for their hearts are in New Orleans.

Diaspora is also used in a more specific way to refer to the scattering of the people of Israel in places far from their homeland. This scattering began in 722 B.C. when the Assyrians conquered the Northern Kingdom (Israel) and moved some of the Israelites to other lands within the Assyrian Empire. More Jews were dispersed during several deportations to Babylonia from the Southern Kingdom (Judah) in the years around 586 B.C. "The Diaspora" (often with a capital *D*) came to refer specifically to exiled Jews, and it is still used today to indicate the aggregate of Jews outside of modern-day Israel.

Whether used of Jews or other groups, however, *diaspora* means more than geographic relocation; it means that the people involved are living in a culture that, at best, is neutral to their identity and values and, at worse, is hostile to them. More often, though, the dominant culture simply offers nothing to sustain the uniqueness of the displaced group. Thus, the greatest threat to the diaspora is *assimilation*—where one's Jewishness or self-concept as a New Orleanian, or whatever, is overpowered by one's identification with the society in which one now lives, and where one's root values are replaced by the values of that society.

Unless you belong to a displaced group, you probably don't think of yourself as part of a diaspora, but if you take your commitment to Christ seriously, there is a sense in which you are. As Christians, we hold citizenship in the kingdom of God, and many of our values derive from that "homeland." Yet we live in a world that cannot be labeled "Christian" in any meaningful way. The culture around us makes it challenging to live a life of faithfulness, for it shares few of our Kingdom values. It often treats Christianity as irrelevant, and it *always* threatens to assimilate us. We can come to feel so "at home" here that God's kingdom seems like a foreign land.

Enter the Bible Story

The Historical Setting

The tale in the Book of Esther is a diaspora story that can be placed in a historical context, but it's best not to read it as actual history. In fact, it probably was never intended to be; rather, it's a compelling story designed to explain the origin of the Jewish festival Purim.

The Esther account is set in the court of a Persian king whom the Bible calls Ahasuerus. Since Ahasuerus is a Hebrew rendering of the Persian title "mighty man," which the actual Persian king Xerxes I (who reigned 486–465 B.C.) used for himself, Ahasuerus is usually assumed to be Xerxes. What's more, the text describes him as ruling "from India to Cush" (1:1), and that jibes with the extent of the Persian Empire in Xerxes' time. (Cush is usually identified with Ethiopia.) The story takes place in the royal city of Susa (1:2), in the southwest part of modern-day Iran, and it begins in "the third year of his rule" (1:3), which would make it 483 B.C., with the main action of the story occurring in "the twelfth year of the rule of King Ahasuerus" (3:7), meaning 474 B.C.

The Jewish population of the empire is described by Haman, the antagonist in the story, as existing "in pockets among the other peoples in the all the provinces of [King Ahasuerus's] kingdom" (3:8). That there was a Jewish diaspora in Susa and throughout the provinces of the empire is not difficult to believe, for once the Persians conquered the Babylonians, who had originally exiled the Judean Jews, that population, now given freedom by the Persians, probably spread throughout the Persian realm in pursuit of job and business opportunities.

But after these basic facts, the historicity of the story falters. It describes Ahasuerus as married first to Vashti and later to Esther. Yet history records that Xerxes was married to Amestris throughout his reign. What's more, queens were chosen from noble Persian families, not from ethnic minorities in the empire. The book portrays Ahasuerus as an easily manipulated fool, but history does not describe Xerxes that way. And while there's a good bit of source material for the Persian era, outside of the Book of Esther itself, no record exists of a mass killing of a large segment of the citizenry at any point in Xerxes' reign, yet that is the central action of the Esther story.

There are also aspects of the story that are almost certainly exaggerations, such as the king throwing a six-month feast, Haman being impaled on a pole seventy-five feet tall, the Jews being permitted to slay seventy-five thousand Persian citizens, and royal edicts that can never be revoked or changed—a practice that would make governing almost impossible.

So the story in the Book of Esther, while in a historical setting, is not history. To say that, however, is not to devalue it or to challenge its place in the Bible or to assume it has nothing of spiritual value. Rather, it is to seek to understand the book for what it is and what role it plays in Scripture. It is fiction, but we should remember that fictional stories often convey truth about humankind. Even more important is that readers in the Persian period were not nearly as concerned as we are to distinguish between *history* and *story*. They valued both and considered that one could carry a holy message as well as the other.

Bible Burlesque

But what kind of fiction is Esther? It's been described a Jewish novella, short story, or wisdom tale, but the fiction-type that best fits the story is *burlesque*, with that being defined as "farcical comedy." One scholar who argues this interpretation is Adele Berlin. She writes, "The Book of Esther is the most humorous of the books in the Bible, amusing throughout and at certain points uproariously funny."[1] While the massacre of thousands is not funny, when it's placed in a story that is made *obviously fictional* by exaggerations, improbabilities, "hyperbole, mockery, and comic misunderstandings and reversals,"[2] it becomes more a storytelling convention than a tragedy report.

The story of Esther is required reading at the annual festival of Purim, still a standard feature of Jewish life today. Purim, based on the deliverance of Jews as told in the Esther story, is not a solemn or somber event, but a celebratory, carnival-like holiday, where a burlesque story fits right in. (See Session 6 for more about Purim.) Berlin writes of the Esther story,

> Its secret identities, gross indulgences, sexual innuendoes, and nefarious plot against the Jews are part and parcel of the carnivalesque world of madness, hilarity, violence, and mock destruction. Indeed, violence is very much a part of this world, and it is in this framework that we should understand the slaughter of the enemies of the Jews. . . . The killing is no more real than anything else in the plot, and is completely in character with the story's carnivalesque nature. . . . The book sets out a threat to the Jews so that the Jewish audience can watch with glee and laugh with relief as it is overcome.[3]

That the story is a burlesque also helps account for the absence of God's name in Esther. Because it's a form of "low comedy," its writer may have felt that the name of the Holy One of Israel ought not to be included, but more likely, God's name was left out because the book establishes the basis for Purim. That festival, unlike Yom Kippur (the Day of Atonement), Sukkoth (the Festival of Booths), and Passover, was not established by

About the Scripture

Talking About God When God Isn't Mentioned

God's name appears nowhere in the Book of Esther, but when Mordecai urges Esther to intervene with the king on behalf of her people, he says, "If you don't speak up at this very important time, relief and rescue will appear for the Jews from another place" (4:14). Some Bible readers have assumed that in saying "from another place," Mordecai was alluding to God. That's possible, but he probably didn't mean that God would act directly to save them in the way that God did when God parted the Red Sea for their ancestors. More likely, Mordecai was simply stating his belief that as God's covenant people, the deliverance of the Jews would occur *somehow*. At present, the only way he could see was for Esther to use her access to the king and speak up. But he didn't think God's purposes would be stymied should Esther refuse.

divine command, and thus the book steers its readers away from such a mistaken conclusion by not mentioning God at all.

The Opening Act (Esther 1–2)

The events in the Book of Esther are kicked off by a royal feast that lasted "six whole months" (1:4b), telegraphing right at the start that what follows is imaginative storytelling. At this event, King Ahasuerus "showed off the awesome riches of his kingdom and beautiful treasures as mirrors of how very great he was" (1:4a). (Comedic hint: This monarch was a fool who equated wealth with prowess.) Then, as if six months of feasting and bragging weren't enough, he threw another bash lasting seven days for everyone in the fortified part of Susa. This meal included an open bar, with "No limits!" (1:8). By the seventh day, "when wine had put the king in high spirits" (1:10), to say nothing of impairing his judgment, he ordered his queen Vashti to make an appearance. This was another way of bragging about himself, showing that in addition to great wealth and fine wine, he also had a beautiful woman at his command.

Vashti, however, refused to be put on display. This angered Ahasuerus, who then sought advice from "certain very smart people" (1:13). (Comedic hint: The king himself wasn't a first-class thinker.) One of his advisers stated that Vashti's refusal should not be tolerated, because when news of it got out, it would make all the women of the empire "look down on their husbands" (1:17). (Comedic hint: The "very smart people" advising the king were insecure fools as well.) This adviser further recommended that the king issue a royal order saying that Vashti would never again come before the king and that her place would be given to "someone better than she" (1:19b). (Comedic hint: "There! That will show her!") This royal decision would be written into the laws of the empire, "laws no one can ever change" (1:19a). The king then sent out "written orders" to all the provinces, translated into the alphabet of each ethnic group in the empire, "that each husband should rule over his own house" (1:22). (Comedic hint: They need a *rule* for that?)

After some time, the king took advice from his male servants that he should select a new queen by means of a search throughout the kingdom for beautiful women. The king should then select the one that pleased him the most (sort of the ancient version of the TV show *The Bachelor*). "The king liked the plan and implemented it" (2:4).

At this point, we meet Mordecai, "a Jew in the fortified part of Susa" (2:5). Unlike Ahasuerus, Mordecai was nobody's fool. We also meet his younger cousin Esther, whom Mordecai had raised after the death of her parents. Esther was beautiful and was swept up by the king's beauty patrol, probably without her consent, along with other "contestants." Taking Mordecai's advice, she did not reveal that she was Jewish.

After viewing the parade of gorgeous women, Ahasuerus chose Esther and set her on a twelve-month course of beauty treatments to make her fit for the king. As king, Ahasuerus had a harem of secondary wives as well, but he "loved Esther more than all the other women; she had won his love and his favor more than all the others. He placed the royal crown on her head and made her ruler in place of Vashti" (2:17).

We now learn that Mordecai performed some sort of work at the king's gate, and in the course of his duties, he happened to overhear two of the king's servants plotting to kill the king. He passed word of this on to Queen Esther, who in turn alerted Ahasuerus. The plot was foiled, the plotters were executed, and a "report about the event was written in the royal record" (2:23).

The Plot Thickens (Esther 3–4)

We next meet Haman, the story's villain. There is less obvious humor in this scene, but one laughable trait is Haman's inflated sense of his own importance. He had a position of authority in the royal court, having been promoted by the king "above all the officials who worked with him" (3:1). Since mention of this promotion comes so soon after Mordecai's saving the king, it may imply that Haman received a promotion that should have been Mordecai's, but that's uncertain. But by command of the king, all the workers at the King's Gate bowed and scraped to Haman—all except Mordecai, that is. Mordecai didn't explain his refusal to his coworkers, but the narrator tells us parenthetically, "He had told them that he was a Jew" (3:4). That doesn't really explain things, however, for while Jews were forbidden to worship other gods, there was no prohibition against a respectful bow to someone for whom one worked. Mordecai's refusal may have sprung from resentment that Haman was promoted over him, but more likely it sprang from a historic enmity between Haman's people and the Benjaminites, the Hebrew tribe to which Mordecai belonged (2:5). Haman was the son of Hammedatha the Agagite (3:1), meaning that he was a descendant of Agag, the Amalekite king mentioned in 1 Samuel 15:8-9 as being spared from death by King Saul. Because this sparing was an act of disobedience against the instruction to kill all the Amalekites, God rejected Saul's kingship of Israel. Saul was a Benjaminite, so subsequent generations of that tribe resented the descendants of Agag.

Whatever the reason, once Haman learned that Mordecai wouldn't bow to him, he resolved to kill not only Mordecai, but all the Jews living under Ahasuerus's rule. He approached the king, asserting that the Jews refused to obey the king's laws. Mordecai, to be sure, had refused to obey the king's command to bow to Haman, but the Jews in general were not resisting the king's laws. Haman requested a royal edict ordering the destruction of the Jews, and sweetened the request by promising an enormous donation to the king's treasuries, an amount almost the equivalent of the annual tribute payments of the entire empire to the king. (Comedic hint: exaggeration.)

Apparently without any thought, the king agreed and issued the necessary proclamation, commanding the citizenry "to wipe out, kill, and destroy all the Jews, both young and old, even women and little children" and "seize their property" (3:13) on a specific date—the thirteenth day of the twelfth month. Haman had picked this day by the casting of dice, called "pur" (3:7).

The king's quick grant of Haman's request reveals another absurdity. To handle the small matter of Vashti's refusal to put in an appearance at a royal party, Ahasuerus consulted with "very smart people" and created a crisis in the monarchy by vacating the queen's throne. But to launch the annihilation of a whole race, he consulted nobody and casually told Haman, "Do as you like with them" (3:11).

Hearing the king's edict, the Jews went into public mourning. Mordecai stood outside the King's Gate, dressed in mourning clothes, with ashes on his head, crying "loudly and bitterly" (4:1). Sheltered as she was in the palace, Esther had not heard the edict, and when she attempted to help Mordecai by sending him everyday clothes so he could enter the King's Gate, he rejected them.

Finally, Mordecai and Esther were able to communicate by means of an intermediary who carried messages between the two. Mordecai told Esther what Haman had done and ordered her to intervene with the king to save her people. In her reply, Esther said nothing about being unwilling, but she raised a practical problem: To go to the king without invitation was a dangerous breach of palace protocol. If the king was so inclined, he could have the uninvited person killed. And Esther had not been called to the king in the past thirty days.

Mordecai's response was stern, telling Esther that even as queen, she was not exempt from the decree against Jews. He said plainly that if she didn't act, help would come for the Jews from some other quarter, but there would be no saving her and her family (that is, Mordecai).

Esther was convinced. She told Mordecai to ask their fellow Jews to fast for three days "to help me be brave," and she pledged that she and her servants would do the same. Esther then said, "Then, even though it's against the law, I will go to the king; and if I am to die, then die I will" (4:16).

While there is less that is obviously funny in this part of the story, the comedic hints given in the first act, along with Haman's pompousness and the king's absurdity in this one, alert audiences that what is threatened against the Jews in this story will not come to pass. Still, in light of the many actual persecutions of Jews, the repeated genocidal actions against Jews at various points in history (and most disastrously in the Holocaust), and the very real anti-Semitism still in many quarters today, laughter needs to remain with *this* story. In real life, genocidal threat toward any people is no laughing matter.

Live the Story

We may think of ourselves as citizens of God's kingdom, but since we've never been there, when it comes to where we *feel* at home, it may well be right here in our earthbound culture. Still, when we accept Christ and the salvation he offers, we eventually find we cannot be faithful to him while embracing every value and way of society. Nonetheless, the culture is seductive and its pull is strong.

Esther models for us what it means to live deeply in a culture without being assimilated by it. When it became important to take a stand on the right side of things, she did so, saying, "If I am to die, then die I will."

It's to be hoped that none of us would ever be put into such a position. But what homeland do your values *and actions* most reflect—this culture or God's kingdom? If you find they are rooted in the former but not in the latter, then what does that call you to do? How can you be more firmly rooted in the values of God's kingdom?

---

[1] Adele Berlin, *The JPS Bible Commentary: Esther* (Philadelphia: The Jewish Publication Society, 2001), xvii.
[2] Berlin, xvi.
[3] Berlin, xxii.

6.

Using Everyday Power to Do Good

Esther 5–10

Claim Your Story

Over whom do you have power? Unless you are a CEO, a military officer, a public official, or hold some other position where people report to you, your top-of-the head response is likely to be, "No one." But that's seldom the conclusion after longer thought. Almost all of us have some power over someone, and often over several someones, even if it's only in the form of influencing another person to do your will.

If, for example, you are a parent of small children, you certainly have the ability to force your children to do quite a few things your way. If you are married, you have a certain amount of power over your spouse. Often in relationships, one partner with the more dominant personality may cause the less dominant partner to comply with his or her wishes without even consciously insisting on it. But in such cases, even the less dominant partner is not powerless. Often, that partner has little ways of getting his or her wishes fulfilled by the other as well. If a friend shares with you something personal about herself, something perhaps embarrassing, and asks you not to repeat it, you suddenly have some power over her, because you could always choose to reveal her secret and thus expose her to embarrassment.

Consider the term *passive-aggressive*. It describes a form of behavior where a person in a seemingly underling position appears to comply with demands of a more powerful, and perhaps even a bullying, individual, but where in reality the person actually resists by such means as procrastination, stubbornness, sullenness, inefficiency, or intentional "mistakes." Passive-aggression is often a form of power wielded by the seemingly powerless.

In any situation involving two or more people, a certain amount of power is present in the dynamics between them. And almost all of us have the power to make someone else feel bad.

As Christians, it's good for us to be aware of how we use the power we have. One thing we can learn from the story in the Book of Esther is that power is best used when we employ it not to build ourselves up, but for the good of others. Esther did that; Mordecai did that; and their people, who were in distress and danger, were delivered. Haman, unfortunately, never learned that lesson, and it cost him dearly.

So, over whom do you have power? What is your intent when you exercise it? How does your use of your power help those who are in difficulty, distress, or danger? How does your use of power reflect your commitment to follow Jesus?

Enter the Bible Story

Haman Gets the Point (Esther 5–7)

Just a reminder: The Book of Esther tells a single story, so in this chapter, we pick up where Chapter 4 left off.

Esther now knew that it was up to her to save her people—the Jews in the Persian Empire—from destruction. To do so, she would have to ask her husband the king to give orders against his own edict, the one that had called for their slaughter. At the same time, she would have to reveal to him that she herself was a Jew. This was a risky undertaking, one that could go badly for her should the king take offense. Chapter 4 ends with her calling for the Jews in Susa to fast for three days while she and her servants did the same. She must have used this time not only to prepare herself emotionally, but also to come up with a plan.

Thus, after those three days, she dressed in her royal garb and took up a position in the inner courtyard of the palace, where Ahasuerus was sure to see her. Thankfully, Ahasuerus was pleased when he noticed her. He extended to her his gold scepter, a signal that she was welcomed to approach him. He recognized that her appearance in the courtyard without being summoned meant she had some request, but he was feeling generous and made a formulaic statement to let her know that: "What do you want? I'll give you anything—even half the kingdom" (5:3). Both he and Esther knew that was hyperbole, however, and was not to be taken literally. It simply meant he was ready to grant her a reasonable request, even if it was something beyond the ordinary. What she asked, however, was only that he attend a feast she had prepared and that he bring Haman with him.

From our viewpoint, it seems strange that Esther didn't immediately tell him what she really wanted, but she was in delicate situation with a volatile, powerful man, and banquets were a common venue for discussing larger requests. It's likely that Ahasuerus realized she had something larger in mind, for when he and Haman went to her meal, the king repeated his "half the kingdom" offer. Again, however, Esther made no mention of her real request but asked that her husband and Haman come to another feast she would prepare for the next day.

In terms of the story, two feasts function to create an interlude between them where Haman's high regard for himself puts him in the ludicrous position of having to honor both personally and publicly the very man who was the central object of his hatred, reminding us again that the genre of this story is farcical comedy—burlesque (see Session 5). Haman left the first feast feeling especially proud. He went home and bragged to his wife and friends that not only had the king promoted him "over the officials and high royal workers" (5:11), but also that he alone had been invited to join the king and queen at a royal feast. The only thing that marred his high spirits, he said, was the view of Mordecai, the man who wouldn't bow to him, sitting at the King's Gate. No problem, said his wife and friends. You're a powerful man in the kingdom. Have "a pointed pole seventy-five feet high" (5:14) set up, and then ask the king to have Mordecai impaled on it. The exaggerated height of this "pole" is another comedic hint: Even if a corpse could be placed on a pole so high and kept upright, no one would be able to see who the offender was. And such a device would be taller than the royal palace in Susa! (Some Bible versions describe this structure as a "gallows," which would still be impractical and ridiculous at such height, but the Hebrew word is better translated as "pole," and impalement was the usual means employed by the Persians to execute enemies). In any case, Haman agreed that this was a wonderful idea, and he ordered that the pole be planted.

That night, the king, having difficulty sleeping, began perusing the royal records. By morning, he came to the notation about Mordecai exposing the plot that would have left the king dead. He realized Mordecai had not been properly recognized for this deed, and learning that Haman was in the courtyard (having come to "tell the king to impale Mordecai" [6:4]), Ahasuerus asked him for advice about what to do for a "man whom the king really wants to honor" (6:6). Not surprisingly, Haman assumed Ahasuerus was talking about him, so he proposed that the honoree be dressed in a royal robe, mounted on a horse the king himself had ridden, and led through the city square by one of the king's officials who would declare aloud, "This is what the king does for the man he really wants to honor!" (6:9).

Then the king, having no idea he was launching an act of poetic justice, ordered Haman to be the official who did this for Mordecai. Haman had no choice but to follow the king's command and ended up honoring Mordecai in the manner he had planned for himself. (We can imagine the audience grinning broadly at this turn of events.) Afterward, Haman hurried home, keeping his head covered to hide his shame.

He returned, however, for Esther's second feast, where the king for a third time made his "half the kingdom" offer to his queen. This time, Esther made her big request: that he spare *her* life and the lives of her people. Until that moment, Ahasuerus had no idea his wife was included in the ethnic group he had ordered annihilated, but Esther was careful to lay no blame on him. She named instead the real villain: Haman. Ahasuerus became so enraged that he left the room to compose himself. While he was gone, Haman, to beg for his life, threw himself on the couch where Esther was reclining. But at that moment, the king returned and accused Haman of attempting to molest her right in the king's palace. (The audience must have been roaring with laughter now.) Then one of the servants helpfully mentioned the pointed pole already erected at Haman's house, and the king ordered that Haman be impaled on it, which was swiftly done.

Across the Testaments

Even Half the Kingdom

Three times, King Ahasuerus offered to give Queen Esther anything she requested, "even half the kingdom" (5:3; 5:6; 7:2). While both Ahasuerus and Esther knew that the phrase did not imply a literal offer of half the kingdom, both understood it was a generous gesture nonetheless and should not be withdrawn simply because the requester asked for something costly. But sometimes kings and other officials found themselves regretting that they had spoken the phrase without due thought. The New Testament gives us an example of that when Herod, probably inebriated but also thrilled after his daughter (or his wife's daughter—the Greek is uncertain) danced at his birthday party. He swore to her, "Whatever you ask I will give to you, even as much as half of my kingdom" (Mark 6:23). What she asked for was the head of John the Baptist. Herod didn't want to kill John but was unwilling to renege on an offer made in front of guests, so he had John executed and his head brought in on plate and given to the young woman.

The Rest of the Story (Esther 8:1–9:19)

This tale now moves to its conclusion. Ahasuerus promptly assigned Haman's property and belongings to Esther and placed on Mordecai's finger the ring signifying that the royal authority that Haman had been given at his promotion a few days earlier was now Mordecai's.

Esther, however, knew that merely getting Haman out of the picture was no victory, for the king's edict against the Jews still stood. Now in tears and bowing at her husband's feet, she asked him to call back the edict. The king, still kindly disposed toward his queen, explained, "Anything written in the name of the king and sealed with the king's royal ring can't be called back" (8:8). It could, however, be met with a counteredict, so Ahasuerus authorized Mordecai to word the necessary document, which would allow the Jews in every location in the empire to join together on the same day that their slaughter was to take place and defend themselves. And where the first edict had been distributed by men on foot who were "fast runners" (3:13), this new one was sent by "riders mounted on royal horses bred from mares known to run fast" (8:10). Hearing this new royal order, some of the non-Jews in land converted to Judaism, "out of fear of the Jews" (8:17).

From here, the story gets bloody, but remember, it's not real. When the fateful day came, many citizens of the empire, following the first edict and no doubt hoping to plunder the property belonging to the Jews, attacked. But the Jews defended themselves vigorously. The storyteller notes that "the tables were turned" (9:1). Fighting occurred throughout the empire, but in Susa alone, the Jews killed five hundred of their attackers, as well as the ten sons of Haman. (There's no mention of whether any Jews are killed.) At the end of the day, the king asked Esther if she had any further requests, and she asked that her people be granted another day to defend themselves against the remaining attackers. The king granted this, and on that second day, the Jews killed another three hundred in Susa. The two-day count of non-Jews killed throughout the whole empire was seventy-five thousand, no doubt another exaggeration for storytelling purposes.

The original edict had directed that those who killed the Jews could also seize their property. The counter-edict gave the same permission to the Jews, but the storyteller is careful to report that when the Jews killed their attackers, they "didn't lay a hand on anything" the people owned (9:10, 15). We're not told why the Jews didn't avail themselves of that provision, but we can see it as a responsible use of their power. Surely many of those killed that day had families who, if the victors seized their property, would have been left homeless and impoverished.

Following the two days of fighting, the Jews throughout the empire held a day of feasting and rejoicing.

Purim Is Established (Esther 9:20-32)

The balance of Chapter 9 explains that at the direction of Mordecai, who was now not only a high official in the Persian court but also a leader among the Jews, the Feast of Purim was established to be held annually on the fourteenth and fifteenth days of Adar (February–March). As we noted in the last chapter, once Haman decided to have the Jews killed, he picked the day for their extermination by the casting of dice, called "pur" (3:7). The day selected was the thirteenth of Adar, which, as we now know, was a day of deliverance for the Jews. The annual celebration of that deliverance, so the storyteller says, received the name "Purim, by using the ancient word *pur*" (9:26). Thus, a main function of the Book of Esther is to explain the origin of that feast.

We mentioned in Chapter 5 that within Judaism, Purim is a celebratory, carnival-like holiday, where the burlesque story of Esther fits right in. Several years ago, the popular American novelist and playwright Herman Wouk, a devout Jew, wrote about Purim in a book about the Jewish faith:

> Purim is the nearest thing Judaism has to a carnival.... The keynote of Purim is riotous rejoicing. The Talmud gives leave to a worshipper to drink on this day until he cannot tell the difference between "Blessed be Mordecai" and "Cursed be Haman."... In Israel a public street festival not unlike Mardi Gras has sprung up, with the name *Ad'lo Yoda*, the Talmud words for "until he cannot tell the difference."[1]

Wouk goes on to explain that Purim is Children's Night in the synagogue, where the reading of the Book of Esther takes place. The children come carrying flags, noisemakers, and traditional whirling rattles called "groggers." The designated person reads from the Scroll of Esther, and each time he comes to the name *Haman*, the children respond loudly. "The name 'Haman' triggers off stamping, pounding, and a hurricane of groggers,"[2] Wouk says, which erupt again each time the villain's name comes up the story.

According to Wouk, beyond this gaiety, Purim includes four religious obligations: to hear the Scroll of Esther read, to distribute charity to the poor, to make a feast, and to exchange gifts with neighbors and friends.[3] The last three of these are mandated in the Book of Esther itself, along with the reason for the holiday: "They are the days on which the Jews finally put to rest the troubles with their enemies. The month is the one when everything turned around for them from sadness to joy, and from sad, loud crying to a holiday. They are to make them days of feasts and joyous events, days to send food gifts to each other and money gifts to the poor" (9:22).

Epilogue (Esther 10)

The final chapter is only three verses long, but it tells us that within the Persian Empire, Mordecai was now "second only to King Ahasuerus in importance" and that he "always wanted to do good things for his Jewish people" (10:3). Once again, we see the responsible use of power—employed for the profit of others rather than for self-aggrandizement.

About the Christian Faith

Power and the Cross

The central symbol of Christianity, the cross, is an emblem of both powerlessness and power. As an instrument of execution, the place where Jesus himself accepted death, it symbolizes his powerlessness. But as an empty cross, one that could not keep Christ dead, it also reminds us of his power over even death. Thus the apostle Paul applied Hosea 13:14 to the work of Christ, writing,

> *Death has been swallowed up by a victory.*
> *Where is your victory, Death?*
> *Where is your sting, Death?* (1 Corinthians 15:54-55)

Live the Story

Those who have studied the dynamics of power say there are six bases from which power can arise.[4] You have power over someone when you:

1. have information needed by the other person (informational power)
2. can punish the other person if he or she does not respond positively (coercion)

3. can provide rewards when a person does respond as you want (reward)
4. have the right to demand a response (authority)
5. are able to move others by your personality force or by psychological manipulation (charisma)
6. can expose the other person to embarrassment or other social costs (blackmail)

Many of the temptations we face in life are ultimately about the *misuse* of power. Much of the harm we do to others is because we've misused our power. Much of the good we do in life is because we've used our power responsibly.

We are usually fooling ourselves when we say we have no power. We're better to recognize what power we have and then consider carefully and prayerfully how and when we use it, so that when we do, we are glorifying God and benefiting someone.

[1] Herman Wouk, *This Is My God* (New York: Doubleday & Company, 1959), 96.
[2] Wouk, 97.
[3] Wouk, 98.
[4] From "Power," *Dictionary of Pastoral Care and Counseling* (Nashville: Abingdon Press, 1990), 932.

Leader Guide

People often view the Bible as a maze of obscure people, places, and events from centuries ago and struggle to relate it to their daily lives. IMMERSION invites us to experience the Bible as a record of God's loving revelation to humankind. These studies recognize our emotional, spiritual, and intellectual needs and welcome us into the Bible story and into deeper faith.

As leader of an IMMERSION group, you will help participants to encounter the Word of God and the God of the Word that will lead to new creation in Christ. You do not have to be an expert to lead; in fact, you will participate with your group in listening to and applying God's life-transforming Word to your lives. You and your group will explore the building blocks of the Christian faith through key stories, people, ideas, and teachings in every book of the Bible. You will also explore the bridges and points of connection between the Old and New Testaments.

Choosing and Using the Bible

The central goal of IMMERSION is engaging the members of your group with the Bible in a way that informs their minds, forms their hearts, and transforms the way they live out their Christian faith. Participants will need this study book and a Bible. IMMERSION is an excellent accompaniment to the Common English Bible (CEB). It shares with the CEB four common aims: clarity of language, faith in the Bible's power to transform lives, the emotional expectation that people will find the love of God, and the rational expectation that people will find the knowledge of God.

Other recommended study Bibles include *The New Interpreter's Study Bible* (NRSV), *The New Oxford Annotated Study Bible* (NRSV), *The HarperCollins Study Bible* (NRSV), the *NIV and TNIV Study Bibles*, and the *Archaeological Study Bible* (NIV). Encourage participants to use more than one translation. *The Message: The Bible in Contemporary Language* is a modern paraphrase of the Bible, based on the original languages. Eugene H. Peterson has created a masterful presentation of the Scripture text, which is best used alongside rather than in place of the CEB or another primary English translation.

One of the most reliable interpreters of the Bible's meaning is the Bible itself. Invite participants first of all to allow Scripture to have its say. Pay attention to context. Ask questions of the text. Read every passage with curiosity, always seeking to answer the basic Who? What? Where? When? and Why? questions.

Bible study groups should also have handy essential reference resources in case someone wants more information or needs clarification on specific words, terms, concepts, places, or people mentioned in the Bible. A Bible dictionary, Bible atlas, concordance, and one-volume Bible commentary together make for a good, basic reference library.

The Leader's Role

An effective leader prepares ahead. This leader guide provides easy-to-follow, step-by-step suggestions for leading a group. The key task of the leader is to guide discussion and activities that will engage heart and head and will invite faith development. Discussion questions are included, and you may want to add questions posed by you or your group. Here are suggestions for helping your group engage Scripture:

State questions clearly and simply.

Ask questions that move Bible truths from "outside" (dealing with concepts, ideas, or information about a passage) to "inside" (relating to the experiences, hopes, and dreams of the participants).

Work for variety in your questions, including compare and contrast, information recall, motivation, connections, speculation, and evaluation.

Avoid questions that call for yes-or-no responses or answers that are obvious.

Don't be afraid of silence during a discussion. It often yields especially thoughtful comments.

Test questions before using them by attempting to answer them yourself.

When leading a discussion, pay attention to the mood of your group by "listening" with your eyes as well as your ears.

Guidelines for the Group

IMMERSION is designed to promote full engagement with the Bible for the purpose of growing faith and building up Christian community. While much can be gained from individual reading, a group Bible study offers an ideal setting in which to achieve these aims. Encourage participants to bring their Bibles and read from Scripture during the session. Invite participants to consider the following guidelines as they participate in the group:

Respect differences of interpretation and understanding.

Support one another with Christian kindness, compassion, and courtesy.

Listen to others with the goal of understanding rather than agreeing or disagreeing.

Celebrate the opportunity to grow in faith through Bible study.

Approach the Bible as a dialogue partner, open to the possibility of being challenged or changed by God's Word.

Recognize that each person brings unique and valuable life experiences to the group and is an important part of the community.

Reflect theologically—that is, be attentive to three basic questions: What does this say about God? What does this say about me/us? What does this say about the relationship between God and me/us?

Commit to a lived faith response in light of insights you gain from the Bible. In other words, what changes in attitudes (how you believe) or actions (how you behave) are called for by God's Word?

Group Sessions

The group sessions, like the chapters themselves, are built around three sections: "Claim Your Story," "Enter the Bible Story," and "Live the Story." Sessions are designed to move participants from an awareness of their own life story, issues, needs, and experiences into an encounter and dialogue with the story of Scripture and to make decisions integrating their personal stories and the Bible's story.

The session plans in the following pages will provide questions and activities to help your group focus on the particular content of each chapter. In addition to questions and activities, the plans will include chapter title, Scripture, and faith focus.

Here are things to keep in mind for all the sessions:

Prepare Ahead

Study the Scripture, comparing different translations and perhaps a paraphrase.

Read the chapter, and consider what it says about your life and the Scripture.

Gather materials such as large sheets of paper or a markerboard with markers.

Prepare the learning area. Write the faith focus for all to see.

Welcome Participants

Invite participants to greet one another.

Tell them to find one or two people and talk about the faith focus.

Ask: What words stand out for you? Why?

Guide the Session

Look together at "Claim Your Story." Ask participants to give their reactions to the stories and examples given in each chapter. Use questions from the session plan to elicit comments based on personal experiences and insights.

Ask participants to open their Bibles and "Enter the Bible Story." For each portion of Scripture, use questions from the session plan to help participants gain insight into the text and relate it to issues in their own lives.

Step through the activity or questions posed in "Live the Story." Encourage participants to embrace what they have learned and to apply it in their daily lives.

Invite participants to offer their responses or insights about the boxed material in "Across the Testaments," "About the Scripture," and "About the Christian Faith."

Close the Session

Encourage participants to read the following week's Scripture and chapter before the next session.

Offer a closing prayer.

1. Help From Surprising Sources
Ezra 1:1–4:5; 4:24–6:22

Faith Focus

God works both through believers and unbelievers to accomplish the divine purposes of redemption and restoration.

Before the Session

On large sheets of paper or posterboard, copy the key dates and events of 539 B.C. to 516 B.C. from the "Ezra-Nehemiah-Esther Chronology" chart on pages 18–20. Display this prominently in your meeting area. (Note: Suggestions for subsequent sessions recommend adding remaining dates and events. You may want to prepare a large version of the entire chart ahead of time and cover portions of it, unveiling appropriate dates and events each time your group gathers.)

Obtain a supply of paper clips to use in the activity in "Live the Story."

Think about an event or experience in your personal life when God worked through someone other than a believer to bring help, healing, and/or hope to you. Plan to tell your group about this experience.

Claim Your Story

Review the writer's story about his wife's pregnancy crisis. Then offer an example from your own life about a time when God used an unlikely person as an answer to your prayers. Ask: Has anything like this ever happened to you? What were the circumstances? What surprised you most about how God answered your prayers? Encourage group members to think broadly across the span of their lives and circumstances.

Point out that in the Book of Ezra, we meet two men, both unbelievers and Persian kings, whom God used to further the divine plan for the people of God.

Enter the Bible Story

Explain that the biblical books of Ezra and Nehemiah describe the restoration of Judah following the Babylonian captivity. The two were originally considered one book and are the final installments in the Old Testament storyline. Briefly review that story, using the key points on pages 10–11. Call attention to the dates and events on the chronological chart you have displayed. Note that Ezra, the narrator, was a priest and a scribe who went to Jerusalem at the direction of the Persian king Artaxerxes.

Introduce Cyrus by asking a volunteer to read aloud his proclamation in Ezra 1:2-4; 6:3-5. Ask someone else to read aloud Isaiah 44:28; 45:1, 13. Ask: How and why was Cyrus good news for God's people exiled in Babylonia? Why do you think he was willing to help them return to their homeland? What were his motives? What similarities and differences do you find between the Ezra and Isaiah accounts about Cyrus? Do you think that the exiles felt any reservations about accepting help from an "outsider"? How do you think you would've felt?

Point out the sizable group—about fifty thousand—of exiles who went to Judah from Babylonia, a trek of some nine hundred miles. Besides appointing Sheshbazzar to lead the group back, Cyrus provided financial resources from the royal treasury to rebuild the Temple in Jerusalem. He also returned treasures and fixtures from the original Temple that the Babylonians had taken at the time they destroyed it. Remind the group that only a small number of those who went to Judah were actually "returnees" and had actually lived in their homeland. Many of the original exiles had died in captivity; most of the exiles had been born in Babylonia.

Note that shortly after they returned to Judah, the former exiles gathered in Jerusalem as an altar was established in the Temple where the original altar had been. Ask: Why was this important? What did it signify? Following the establishment of the altar, the people celebrated the Festival of Booths, and about seven months later, reconstruction of the Temple began.

Using the information in "Facing Opposition" (pages 15–16), explain the differences between the Jews now living in Judah, including their worship practices. Then ask a volunteer to read aloud Ezra 4:1-5. Ask: What was behind the request in verse 2? Why was it immediately dismissed by the former exiles? Point out that at this point because of opposition, work on the Temple reconstruction stopped and did not resume for ten years.

Call attention to the account of the resumption of the Temple construction in Ezra 4:24, and note the role of Haggai and Zechariah. Also highlight the roles of the Persian king, Darius, and his official, Tattenai, as told in Ezra 5–6. Note that the Temple was completed and dedicated in 516 B.C., after which the restored community gathered to observe Passover. Read aloud Ezra 6:16, 22.

Live the Story

Display a paper clip and ask: When was the last time you used one of these? What did you use it for?

After a few responses, suggest that this common item actually has a number of purposes other than holding together loose pieces of paper. A paper clip can tightly close up a bag containing chips, cereal, or other foods. It can function as a zipper pull when one unexpectedly breaks off. It can be straightened and used to "unpop" the lock on a bathroom door. It makes a great hanger for a Christmas tree ornament. And it is just the right size for pressing the electronic reset buttons on various devices.

Remind the group that God sometimes uses people in unexpected and surprising ways too in order to accomplish the divine plan. God used two pagan Persian kings, Cyrus and Darius, to help God's people leave captivity, return to Judah, and worship again in Jerusalem.

Give each person a paper clip as a reminder that God works in creative and often surprising ways in our lives, and God's plans will not be derailed. Ask them to attach their paper clips to their Bibles or put them in another place where they will see them regularly and remember the surprising ways God acts. Close in prayer, asking God to keep you open to the many ways God chooses to work. Pray that God will use you to help answer the needs and prayers of others.

2. Embodying God's Law
Ezra 4:6-23; 7:1–10:44

Faith Focus

As people of faith, we accept Ezra's challenge to study God's law, teach it to others, and embody it in our lives.

Before the Session

As suggested in Session 1, on large sheets of paper or posterboard, copy the key dates and events of 486 B.C. to 458–457 B.C. from the "Ezra-Nehemiah-Esther Chronology" chart on pages 18–20. Display this prominently in your meeting area. (Or, if you prepared the entire chart earlier, uncover these dates and events.)

On colorful cardstock or pieces of construction paper, print in large, bold letters the following, one per sheet: "Proclaimer," "Ascertainer," "Explainer," "Framer." Attach these to the walls around your meeting area.

Obtain enough sheets of paper (any size or kind) for each person in your group to have one.

Claim Your Story

Begin by asking group members to recall the first Bible story they remember hearing. If they seem reluctant to speak up, give a personal example. Ask: What was the story? Who told it? What do you remember most about the story? Since that time, what additional truths about God have you learned as you have heard sermons and discussions about that particular Scripture?

Affirm group members' commitment to knowing more about what the Bible says and how to apply it to their lives by their participation in your group. Then call attention to the four words displayed on the walls: "Proclaimer," "Ascertainer," "Explainer," "Framer." Explain briefly their meanings. Ask group members to stand beside the word that best describes their current role in relationship to the Bible. Ask: What would you need to do to assume the other roles? Are you willing to do those things? Read aloud the questions at the end of "Claim Your Story" on page 22, pausing briefly between each question.

Enter the Bible Story

Ask: Have you ever been falsely accused of something? What were the circumstances? How did you respond? How did the false accusations affect you and your plans?

Explain that the restored community of Jews in Judah faced just such charges. Call attention to the dates and events on the chronological chart you have displayed and to details in Ezra 4:6-23. Briefly explain the reason for studying this event in connection with the events described in Chapters 7–10. Note the highlights of the letter of indictment, the king's reply, and the effect this had on the rebuilding work.

Ask a volunteer to read aloud Ezra 7:10. Briefly explain Ezra's roles as priest and scribe. Then ask: In which role did Ezra want to return to Judah? Why do you think King Artaxerxes so readily agreed to Ezra's request to be allowed to take a delegation there? Why was it so important to Ezra to make this trip?

Note that King Artaxerxes went well beyond Ezra's request, not only allowing him to return to Judah with a delegation of exiles, but also sending with them a letter authorizing Ezra to lead religious reforms and name judges and supervisors among the Jews. In addition, he gave Ezra authority to draw funds from the royal treasury and the empire treasuries in the area known as "Beyond the River." Even though he had halted the rebuilding work in Jerusalem, King Artaxerxes played a significant and positive role in the lives of the returning exiles, much like Kings Cyrus and Darius I had done. Ask: Whom did Ezra credit for all of this? (See 7:27.)

Note the listing of male members of the delegation in Chapter 8. With women and children, the delegation likely numbered 5,000–6,000 people. Remind the group of the hazards the delegation would face. Then read aloud 8:21-23. Ask: Why do you think Ezra felt this fast for their safety was necessary when he had the letter from the king? Why did he not request a bodyguard from the king? Point out what the delegation did once they had safely arrived.

Ask a volunteer to read aloud Deuteronomy 7:3-4. Then lead the group to identify and discuss "The Communal Problem" by asking such questions as these: What was the real issue behind the problem of intermarriage? Who in the community was involved? What was Ezra's concern? What implications did intermarriage have for God's people?

As time permits, read aloud all or selected verses from Ezra's prayer in 9:6-15. Note the community's response and the solution at which they arrived. Acknowledge that this is one of the Bible's "difficult" texts. Modern readers struggle with what was required of God's people here in light of our understanding of God and God's love for the world. Note the harsh consequences this covenant had on the women and children who were sent away. Encourage group members to express their insights and feelings about what happened and why it was determined to be necessary.

Live the Story

Affirm that while we struggle with what God's people did in order to show their desire for God to restore them, they were right to understand that something radical was necessary. God had called them not just to learn the law, but to embody it, and they had failed miserably. Suggest that the same principle applies to us. When we have turned away from God and have begun to do things that keep us separated from God, we too must take drastic steps to show that we are sincere in wanting God to restore our relationship.

Remind the group of the writer's suggestion of a "rip-out list," and explain what that means. Read aloud the next-to-last paragraph on page 28; then read aloud the questions in the last paragraph on page 29. Give each person a sheet of paper and ask participants to think of things in their lives that they need to "rip out" in order for God to restore them to a right relationship. Allow a few moments of quiet reflection. Then ask them, as a symbol of their commitment to learning and living the Bible's teachings in a right relationship with God, to rip their pieces of paper and place them on the floor in the center of the group. Close with prayer, asking God to help you ascertain what the Word of God says and "frame it," putting its precepts into practice in your life.

3. Dealing With Opposition
Nehemiah 1:1–7:73a

Faith Focus

When doing the work of the Lord, we, like Nehemiah, encounter opposition. But God remains faithful to God's promises.

Before the Session

As suggested in Session 1, on large sheets of paper or posterboard, copy the remaining key dates and events from the "Ezra-Nehemiah-Esther Chronology" chart on pages 18–20. Display this prominently in your meeting area. (Or, if you prepared the entire chart earlier, uncover these dates and events.)

Enlist two people from your group to narrate and enact the dialogue between Nehemiah and the king in Nehemiah 2:1-8. The Common English Bible translation is especially clear and good for this purpose.

Before group members arrive, use overturned chairs, tables, boxes, books, and other items to block the entrance to your meeting room or area. Use caution in stacking and arranging the items, but arrange them in such a way that makes entry impossible without moving them.

Claim Your Story

As group members arrive, stand aside and observe their reactions to the blocked access to your meeting area. Make no attempts to assist or answer questions at first. After several group members have arrived, and if no one has attempted to remove the obstruction, suggest that you work together to do so. Again, use caution in moving the items, and return them to their proper locations.

After group members have assembled in your meeting area, debrief this experience by asking such questions as: What thoughts came to your mind when you saw that our meeting area was obstructed? What did you do? Why? Were you tempted just to walk away and go home? Why or why not? What motivated you to remove the obstacles blocking your way?

Suggest that this lighthearted exercise can help us consider more serious obstacles we face when we are doing what we perceive to be God's work and God's will. Summarize the account of the youth center idea that received strong opposition from "Claim Your Story" (pages 31–32). Ask the questions the writer offers in the next-to-last paragraph on page 32, and allow group members time to reflect and respond. After everyone has had an opportunity to do so, introduce Nehemiah as someone who can help you further consider these questions.

Enter the Bible Story

Summarize what we know about Nehemiah from "The Man, the Time, and the Place" (pages 32–33). Call attention to dates and events from the chronological chart. Note that we have no reason to believe that Nehemiah had ever been to Jerusalem, yet for him and for the other exiles, it was the center of their ethnic and faith identity. When Nehemiah learned from his brother Hanani about the conditions in Jerusalem, he felt an even greater pull to his ancestral home and devised a plan that might allow him to go.

Read aloud key verses from Nehemiah's prayer in 1:5-11. Then ask the two group members you previously enlisted to enact the dialogue in 2:1-8 that reveals Nehemiah's plan to go to Judah. Ask: Why was it so important for Nehemiah to go to Jerusalem? Why was his plan so risky? What could've happened to him if things had not gone his way? Remind the group of the actions one hundred years earlier of the Persian king Cyrus in allowing exiles to go to Judah. Now another Persian king, Artaxerxes, agreed that Nehemiah and others could travel there to rebuild Jerusalem, going even so far as to provide directives for their building supplies and appointing Nehemiah as governor of Judah. Note Nehemiah's acknowledgement of God's activity in this situation in 2:8.

Suggest that we might assume that things would go smoothly for Nehemiah from this point. With letters from the king ensuring safe passage and a military escort, Nehemiah and company journeyed and arrived safely in Jerusalem. But they were not there long before they met opposition in the form of Sanballat and Tobiah. Ask the group to help you draw a verbal portrait of these two men and explain why they were opposed to the city walls being rebuilt. Describe the various things they did to prevent construction of the walls and how Nehemiah dealt with their threats and plots. Also recall the additional obstacle Nehemiah faced within the faith community. Ask a volunteer to read aloud Exodus 22:25-27 to show the seriousness of the problem. Then explain how Nehemiah handled the situation.

Stress that in spite of the repeated efforts of Sanballat, Tobiah, and Geshem to thwart the rebuilding project and the problem within the Israelite community, the wall was completed in fifty-two days. Yet even that did not end the efforts of those opposing Nehemiah. Still, Nehemiah was not deterred. The wall was completed, the gates were hung, gatekeepers and guard were installed to control access into the city, and God's people began returning to build houses inside the walls. Ask: What do you think kept Nehemiah strong in the face of all the opposition he faced? What prevented him from giving up?

Live the Story

Acknowledge that Nehemiah never won over his opponents, yet in spite of that, he was convinced that God was on his side and would help him and remain faithful. Remind the group of the questions the writer posed at the beginning of this session about dealing with resistance and facing opposition, and ask them to recall their responses. Ask: What does Nehemiah's example teach us about how to live faithfully and do the will and work of God in such situations?

Close by leading group members in a directed prayer such as this: Lord, I thank you for your faithfulness to me, even when I am unfaithful to you. I acknowledge that I sometimes want to give up and walk away when I face opposition in my work for you. Strengthen me when I grow weak. Give me discernment to know what you want me to do as a part of Christ's body, the church. Show me how best to use the qualities and resources you have given me in partnership with others in the Body to build and grow your kingdom on earth. In Jesus' name I pray. Amen.

4. Hearing and Doing

Nehemiah 7:73b–13:31

Faith Focus

As faithful believers, we accept the challenge of Ezra and Nehemiah to seek out areas in our lives that call for renewed commitment to and reformed practice of the faith.

Before the Session

Gather a number of instruction manuals or booklets for various household items (appliances, computers, cell phones, games, tools, equipment, and so forth). You might also include "how-to" books if you have any on hand. Take these to the session.

Claim Your Story

Display the various manuals, booklets, and books that you have gathered and ask: What do these items have in common? Hold up a few of them, one at a time, and ask: What might we expect to know how to do from reading this? Continue this line of questioning for a couple of minutes.

Move beyond the obvious responses to stress that in order to use any of the items or do any of the things explained in the "how-to" books, we must do more than simply read the manuals. We must follow the instructions carefully and apply what we read. Suggest that the same is true with the Bible. It is one thing to read it, hear a sermon based on it, or participate in a Bible study. It is quite another to apply the teachings of the Bible personally and in a manner that changes the way we live in relationship to God and to others.

Read aloud the questions from "Claim Your Story" on page 42, pausing briefly after each question. Allow group members time to reflect on these questions for a few moments.

Enter the Bible Story

Note that for the Israelite community, "the Instruction scroll from Moses," or Torah, was their instruction guide for living as the chosen people of God. It was their "how-to" guide. They understood it to be God's divine will for them and saw it as their source of life.

Briefly explain the questions scholars have surrounding the placement of Nehemiah 8–10. Then set the stage for the events recorded in these chapters. Stress that the people, rather than Ezra, initiated the reading of the Instruction scroll, and for many, this was probably the first time they had actually heard it, although they knew of its existence from their parents, grandparents, and other community elders. Then ask: What was the people's response when they first heard the reading from the Instruction scroll? Why do you think they reacted the way they did? What did Ezra, Nehemiah, and the Levites say to the people when they saw their reaction? What did the people do next?

Emphasize that *hearing* resulted in *doing* on the part of the people of Judah. After celebrating the Festival of Booths, they observed a day of repentance, which included more reading from the Instruction scroll, confession, and worship of God. Note the prayer in 9:5b-37, and outline what it includes (praise of God, recitation of God's mighty acts, admission of the sins of the people's ancestors, recognition that God had not forsaken their ancestors, the people's wrongdoing, God's persistent faithfulness, the people's present circumstances, and what lead up to their domination by foreign powers). As time permits, read aloud portions of this prayer.

Call attention to the people's written pledge to follow the Instruction. Ask volunteers to read aloud key verses such as 9:38 and 10:28-29. Highlight what the pledge involved by asking group members to call out specifics from 10:30-39. Point out that those things from the Instruction to which the people committed to live were related to racial exclusiveness and ceremonial obligations. Ask: Why do you think these parts of the Instruction were particularly significant to the people? What did obedience to these instructions insure?

Remind the group that the Babylonians' destruction to Jerusalem in 586 B.C. was massive. Though the wall had now been rebuilt, the city remained uninhabited because there was nowhere for the people to live inside the walls. Briefly summarize the process used in determining how the city would be repopulated as described in Chapter 11. Note the listings of priests and Levites in 12:1-26, and point out the details that follow describing how the "work" of the Temple would continue.

Following the reading of the Instruction, people's repentance, their pledge to live according to the Instruction, the decisions concerning repopulation of

Jerusalem, and dedication of the rebuilt city wall, Nehemiah returned to Babylonia to give a report to King Artaxerxes. The king apparently then sent him back to Judah for another term as governor. Explain what had transpired during Nehemiah's absence (abuse of Temple space by Tobiah, lack of support for the Levites, exchange of commerce on the Sabbath, intermarriage). Note Nehemiah's response to the community's failure to keep their religious commitments during his absence.

Live the Story

Affirm the example the post-exilic community provides for us in that they heard the word of God, renewed their commitment to follow God's instructions for them, and reformed their behaviors and lifestyles to demonstrate that commitment. Acknowledge that even those who grew less faithful to their commitments by the close of the Book of Nehemiah can serve a positive purpose for us in that they remind us of the necessity and importance of maintaining and cultivating our relationship with God.

Ask group members to close their eyes and consider their personal responses as you read aloud the questions in the last paragraph on page 49. Lead the group in prayer, asking God to show you the areas in your lives that reflect unfaithfulness and lack of commitment. Pray for courage to take decisive steps to act on the things God reveals to you.

5. The Diaspora
Esther 1–4

Faith Focus

As believers, we learn from Esther how to live a life of faithfulness in the midst of a culture that shares few of our values, sometimes treats us as irrelevant, and threatens to assimilate us.

Before the Session

Using the Internet, research and print out several stories and articles about individuals who were displaced from their homes in New Orleans and other Gulf Coast cities following Hurricanes Katrina and Rita. If possible, find initial stories about individuals and families and later follow-up, "where are they now" accounts. Collect enough different stories so that you can divide your group into smaller subgroups for discussion. If you prefer not to divide into subgroups, select one such story and plan to summarize it for your group, answering the questions suggested below.

Or, if you have a group member who was personally affected by one of these tragedies or who had family members who were displaced by it, ask this person ahead of time to share this experience with the group. Offer the questions at the top of page 86 for consideration as he or she plans to say.

Also obtain two empty bottles or small jars with lids, a small amount of vegetable oil, and some salt. Just before your session begins, fill the two bottles or jars about 2/3 with water.

Claim Your Story

Begin by dividing your group into smaller subgroups. Give each subgroup an article or collection of articles about an individual or family displaced by Hurricane Katrina and/or Rita. Ask the subgroups to review the stories and be prepared to summarize them for the larger group. Or, review together the article you obtained. If instead of gathering articles you enlisted someone to provide a personal account of their experiences, call for that report at this time.

After about ten minutes, reassemble the subgroups and call for summary reports from each about their assigned individual or family. Encourage the subgroups to provide answers to questions such as these: How did the individuals evacuate? What were they able to take with them? Where did they go? How long did they stay there? What challenges did they face? Where did they finally settle? If they did not return to their hometown, what factors led to that decision? If they were able to return, what made that possible? Where do they consider "home"?

Suggest that this disastrous event serves as a contemporary example of "diaspora." Explain what this term means generally and then specifically to the people of Israel. Note the dispersions of Israelites from the Northern Kingdom (Israel) in 722 B.C. and from the Southern Kingdom (Judah) beginning in 586 B.C. Encourage group members to identify, based on their individual reading, what such dispersions threatened to do to the Israelite people, their culture, their identity, and their values.

Next, display one of the bottles or jars of water, and add to it a small amount of vegetable oil. Close the lid tightly and shake it; then hold it again before the group. Add salt to the other bottle or jar of water, close the lid, and shake it thoroughly. Point out the obvious: The oil was not mixed or "assimilated" into the water, while the salt was. Stress that assimilation into the dominating culture was the biggest threat the Israelites faced from the Diaspora. Whether the dominating culture was simply neutral or was openly hostile toward them, nothing existed in their new environment that would help them nurture and sustain their uniqueness. Suggest that as Christians, we too face such a challenge as citizens of God's kingdom. Read aloud the "Faith Focus" statement on page 85.

Enter the Bible Story

Set the story from the Book of Esther in both its historical and its biblical contexts. Identify Ahasuerus and Xerxes I. Remind the group that Diaspora Jews were living in Susa, where the story in Esther is set. Carefully explain the reasons the writer says that it is best not to read the Book of Esther as actual history. Note the differences between the historical facts about Xerxes and Vashti and the biblical accounts of Ahasuerus and Vashti. Ask group members to recall from their reading the incidents of exaggerations and humor in the biblical story. Then ask: So what kind of book is Esther? How should we read the story? What is its role in the Bible? Does it disturb you that biblical scholars and writers identify the Book of Esther as fiction? Why or why not? How do you identify or describe it?

Remind the group about the role of the story of Esther in the Jewish festival of Purim. Read aloud the statements on page 54 from scholar Adele Berlin. Point out that the festival of Purim was not established by divine command like the Jewish holy days of Yom Kippur, Sukkoth, and Passover, and that God's name is not mentioned at all in the Book of Esther. Ask group members to suggest reasons for that obvious omission. Ask: Why would such a story be especially meaningful to Diaspora Jews? to Jews today?

Encourage the group to help you summarize and retell the events recorded in Esther 1–2, noting especially the verses that reflect exaggeration and humor. Continue retelling the unfolding story with the events in Esther 3–4. Ask: At what points does this story become humorous and/or far-fetched to you? Why? What risks did Esther face if she did what Mordecai told her to do? What would have happened if she had refused?

Ask group members to paint verbal portraits of the various characters in the story: King Ahasuerus, Queen Vashti, Haman, Mordecai, Esther. Guide their characterizations by considering such questions as these: How did this person see himself or herself? How did others see him or her? What motivated this person's actions?

Live the Story

Ask group members to identify the place they consider "home." Where is the one place they feel most at home? Why? What is it about this place that makes this the case?

Next, ask them to identify a place where they have felt as though they did not belong. What about that place caused or causes them to feel that way? How, and how well, did they function in that place?

Suggest that as Christians—followers of Christ and citizens of God's kingdom—our present world and contemporary culture, though familiar to us, are not our real home. If we find ourselves never at odds with our culture and its seductions, we should consider whether we are being assimilated by it and determine the changes we need to make in our lives to reverse that trend.

Display again the two bottles or jars and shake them. Then read aloud the last paragraph from "Live the Story" on page 59. Close with a prayer asking God to give you the courage always to take a stand on the right side of things in a culture that often promotes the wrong side as ideal and preferable.

6. Using Everyday Power to Do Good
Esther 5–10

Faith Focus

As believers, we can model Esther and Mordecai's responsible use of power to bring about beneficial results for those in difficulty, distress, or danger.

Before the Session

Gather party decorations and supplies such as colorful flags; paper streamers; balloons; rattles, whistles, and other noisemakers; and paper plates, cups, and napkins. As much as possible, use items you and others have left over from other events. Enlist a few group members to help you ahead of time to decorate your meeting room or area. Ask other group members to bring beverages, snacks, finger foods, and dessert items. Plan a celebration as your group concludes this short-term study and you learn more about the Jewish festival of Purim.

Contact group members ahead of time and encourage them to bring nonperishable food items for your church's food pantry or your local food bank. Remind them that such an act is one of the religious obligations of the Jewish festival of Purim.

Plan to relate the story of Esther as if you are telling it to those who are hearing it for the first time. Review the biblical text from Chapters 1–4 and the preceding session in this book. Then thoroughly review the remainder of the biblical account and the related material in this book. If you prefer, enlist someone in your group or in your congregation who is a gifted storyteller and ask him or her to come to your group to tell the story of Esther, Ahasuerus, Mordecai, and Haman. If you enlist someone for this purpose, provide him or her with a copy of this book.

Claim Your Story

Begin by dividing group members into pairs or small groups, and assign to each pair or small group one of these categories: Marriage/Family, Peer/Friendship, School/Educational, Work/Corporate, Government, Religion. Ask each pair or small group to discuss and be prepared to explain a scenario from their assigned category in which power was abused or misused. They can recall an historical event, suggest a recent or current situation making headlines, or create a scenario using their imaginations. Allow the pairs or small groups several minutes to work together. Then call for reports from each. In each example, lead the pair or small groups to determine: who held the power, how the power was misused or abused, who was hurt as a result, and how the individuals or groups involved could have used power for good rather than for personal gain or harm to others.

Ask group members to consider the question, Over whom do you have power? Affirm that the story from the Book of Esther reminds us that we best use power not to build ourselves up but for the good of others. Read aloud the questions in the last paragraph of "Claim Your Story" on page 62.

Enter the Bible Story

Remind group members that the Book of Esther tells a single story, and its purpose is to explain the origin of the Jewish festival called Purim. Using the information in "Purim Is Established" (pages 66–68), remind adults about Purim and how it is celebrated. Read aloud the comments from Herman Wouk, and offer his additional explanation of Children's Night in the synagogue during Purim. Explain that you will simulate this occasion as you review and conclude your study of the Book of Esther.

Display the rattles, whistles, and other noisemakers you brought and ask each person to choose one. Explain to participants that they will hear the story from the Book of Esther, and in keeping with the Purim tradition when Jewish children hear this story, they are to use their noisemaker each time they hear the name *Haman*.

Introduce the guest storyteller, if you have one, and begin (or ask your guest storyteller to begin) by reviewing and summarizing the events from Esther 1–4. Then, in more detail, tell the rest of the story, using the biblical account and the information in this book. Remind group members to use their noisemakers each time they hear the name *Haman*. Suggest that if they feel silly doing so, they should remember the celebratory nature of the Jewish festival of Purim and the great relief and happiness the Jews in the story of Esther felt when they were delivered from Haman's genocidal plot. In telling the story, stress the following:

- Esther's plan and the risks she took in approaching King Ahasuerus with her request
- the king's repeated and exaggerated promise to give Esther "half the kingdom"
- Haman's self-aggrandizement and his disdain of Mordecai
- the king's act that brought "poetic justice" to Mordecai and shame to Haman
- how Haman's true nature was exposed
- the irony of Haman being impaled on the pole he had erected for that purpose for Mordecai and of the king then giving Mordecai the authority and position Haman had once held
- the king's counter-edict and its results
- the establishment of the Feast of Purim, how it got its name, and the four religious obligations cited by Herman Wouk

Read aloud Esther 10:1-3 and note Mordecai's responsible and selfless use of power. Ask group members to identify other points in the story at which Mordecai, Esther, and King Ahasuerus used their power for good and to help those who were in difficulty, distress, and danger.

Live the Story

Call attention to the six bases from which power can arise as cited on pages 68–69. Review them one by one, and for each, ask group members to offer an example or scenario that illustrates it. Encourage them, if they are comfortable doing so, to offer personal examples, as appropriate. In each case, lead the group to determine how power can be used in the situation for good rather than for harm or for selfish purposes. Suggest that each time we find ourselves in a situation in which we "hold the power," we have choices to make. We must decide whether we will misuse or abuse the power or whether we will use it responsibly and for the good of others.

Offer a prayer such as this: God, we acknowledge that you have entrusted to each of us power and influence over situations and over other people. We confess that we sometimes misuse and abuse this power by controlling others through bullying, procrastination, stubbornness, and other selfish behaviors.

We ask your forgiveness. We also ask that you would show us how best to use the power at our disposal so that we reflect our commitment to follow Jesus and help others who are distressed, in danger, or facing difficult situations.

Following the prayer, encourage a time of celebration and fellowship. Remind group members that the Feast of Purim is a time of celebration. Suggest that we too have many reasons to celebrate God's deliverance of us and faithfulness and goodness to us. Collect the food items that group members have brought and make arrangements for their delivery to the distribution site.

IMMERSE YOURSELF IN ANOTHER VOLUME
IMMERSION
Bible Studies

Genesis	9781426716232
Exodus, Leviticus, Numbers	9781426716324
Deuteronomy	9781426716331
Joshua, Judges, Ruth	9781426716348
1 & 2 Samuel, 1 & 2 Kings, 1 & 2 Chronicles	9781426716355
Ezra, Nehemiah, Esther	9781426716362
Job	9781426716300
Psalms	9781426716294
Proverbs, Ecclesiastes, Song of Solomon	9781426716317
Isaiah, Jeremiah, Lamentations	9781426716379
Ezekiel, Daniel	9781426716386
Hosea, Joel, Amos, Obadiah, Jonah	9781426716393
Micah, Nahum, Habakkuk, Zephaniah, Haggai, Zechariah, Malachi	9781426716409
Apocrypha	9781426742972
Matthew	9781426709821
Mark	9781426709166
Luke	9781426709838
John	9781426709845
Acts	9781426709852
Romans	9781426709869
1 & 2 Corinthians	9781426709876
Galatians, Ephesians, Philippians	9781426710841
Colossians, 1 & 2 Thessalonians	9781426710858
1 & 2 Timothy, Titus, Philemon	9781426709906
Hebrews	9781426709890
James; 1 & 2 Peter; 1, 2 & 3 John; Jude	9781426709883
Revelation	9781426709920

Available at Cokesbury and other booksellers   AbingdonPress.com